OUR BODIES
TELL
GOD'S STORY

OUR BODIES TELL GOD'S STORY

Discovering the Divine Plan
for Love, Sex, and Gender

CHRISTOPHER WEST

BrazosPress
a division of Baker Publishing Group
Grand Rapids, Michigan

Published by Brazos Press
a division of Baker Publishing Group
PO Box 6287, Grand Rapids, MI 49516-6287
www.brazospress.com

Printed in the United States of America

Library of Congress Cataloging-in-Publication Data
Names: West, Christopher, 1969– author.
Title: Our bodies tell God's story : discovering the divine plan for love, sex, and gender / Christopher West.
Description: Grand Rapids : Brazos Press, a division of Baker Publishing Group, 2020. | Includes index.
Identifiers: LCCN 2019017966 | ISBN 9781587434273 (pbk.)
Subjects: LCSH: Sex—Religious aspects—Christianity. | Human body—Religious aspects—Christianity. | Catholic Church—Doctrines.
Classification: LCC BT708 .W424 2020 | DDC 233/.5—dc23
LC record available at https://lccn.loc.gov/2019017966

ISBN 978-1-58743-461-7 (casebound)

20 21 22 23 24 25 26   7 6 5 4 3 2 1

In keeping with biblical principles of creation stewardship, Baker Publishing Group advocates the responsible use of our natural resources. As a member of the Green Press Initiative, our company uses recycled paper when possible. The text paper of this book is composed in part of post-consumer waste.

CONTENTS

FOREWORD

Eric Metaxas

In case anyone has missed it, the Western church is facing a serious reckoning with its inability to respond effectively to the secular world's challenges regarding the meaning of sex, gender, marriage, and the family. And what could be more central to human life than the meaning of these most central of human concepts? The popular culture has been telling us a saccharine, rainbow-hued fairy tale about our bodies and about human love that innumerable people have nonetheless found more compelling and appealing than anything they've probably ever heard in church. But it strikes me—and the author of this wonderful book—that that is because we in the church haven't been properly equipped to understand that our bodies tell a true story that is more glorious and transcendent and powerful and multidimensional and resonant and satisfying than we've ever imagined. As Christopher West illuminates for us in this much-needed and timely work, our bodies tell *God's* story.

The Enlightenment has taught us an infinity of things about the workings of the human body as a biological organism. But when it comes to the deepest meaning of our creation as male and female, the Enlightenment, ironically, has left us fumbling in the dark. It tells a story that is ultimately reductionist and that is therefore only part of the larger and grander story; and in being only part of the larger story but purporting to be the whole story, it is what we might accurately call a "lie" and a "fiction." The body is not only biological. To say that we are only biological is like saying that Albert Einstein and Mother Teresa and Mozart were only clumps of cells. As West correctly asserts, "Since we're made in the image of God as male and female, the body . . . is also *theological*. It tells an astounding divine story. . . . This means that when we get the body and sex wrong, we get the divine story wrong as well."

Could this possibly explain why embracing the values of the sexual revolution has coincided with a widespread loss of biblical faith in general? "Sex is not just about sex," posits West. "The way we understand and express our sexuality points to our deepest-held convictions about who we are, who God is, who Jesus is, what the church is (or should be), the meaning of love, the ordering of society, and the mystery of the universe."

These are bold claims, but they are also indisputably and powerfully and dramatically true. And if you read this book you will see that West backs them up so that we can all see how true and inescapable they are. Of course these are not just his ideas. His task in this first-of-its-kind book is to make accessible for a broad Christian readership the insights of someone whom many consider the greatest Christian leader of the twentieth century. In my book *Seven Men: And the Secret of Their Greatness*, I wrote that there is much to be said for the view that that title belongs to the man who led the world's Catholics into the twenty-first century: John Paul II. Christian history will surely remember him for his fearless witness to Christ in the face of state-sponsored atheism (he was one of the key figures in the collapse of communism across Europe); for his tireless efforts in building bridges across denominational lines (he even reached out to Protestant and Orthodox Christians, asking them to help him reenvision the papacy); and for his courageous defense of the dignity of human life in the face of powerful ideological threats against it.

Today, however, as Christians in the culture and in their own congregations and families continue to grapple—and sometimes fail to grapple—with the near total eclipse of the biblical meaning of sex, gender, and marriage, it's becoming increasingly evident that John Paul II's greatest legacy may prove to be an extensive collection of biblical reflections he gave on the theology of the human body. This bold, compelling, hopeful, and healing vision of our creation as male and female has been hailed by Catholics and Protestants alike as an antidote to the sexual crisis now plaguing the church and the world. For that antidote to spread, however, the keen insights of these dense and scholarly lectures need to be put in a language that average believers can understand.

Which brings us back to Christopher West and the happy gift of this book.

West began teaching John Paul II's Theology of the Body to a primarily Catholic audience in the mid-1990s—efforts that soon found him authoring bestselling books and lecturing around the globe. When a committee at Focus on the Family charged with drafting an official statement on sexuality solicited West's assistance in the early 2000s, West took up the task of translating John Paul II's biblical reflections for believers who would rarely (if ever) pick up something authored by a pope. Having been raised Catholic but evangelized largely by Protestant believers during his college years, West is fluent in both languages, so to speak, which makes him the perfect candidate to write this book. In his introduction, West mentions the debt of gratitude he feels toward his Protestant brothers and sisters for inspiring him with their commitment to Christ and their love for God's Word. As you enter more and more into this study of God's Word, you will surely agree with me that we also owe him our gratitude for making John Paul II's Theology of the Body accessible and relatable to the whole body of Christ.

INTRODUCTION

There is really no way to overstate the profound impact [the Theology of the Body has] had on my mind and my soul. It helped me see how profound Christianity is in answering the deepest questions we all have about who we are and how we are called to relate to others and to God . . . by showing how the physical and spiritual are united in a profound way in our Lord Jesus Christ.

—Glenn Stanton

I gave my life to Jesus when I was twenty years old. I had been raised a Catholic and did the "Catholic thing" growing up. Unfortunately, like so many other Catholics, I hadn't had an interior conversion to Christ. Jesus was a religious "idea" to me, a historical figure, and, I suppose, a holy teacher (whatever that meant). But I didn't know him personally as my Savior until, largely through the influence of Protestant teachers and preachers, I started studying the Bible in my college years and experienced a dramatic conversion of heart.

Without a doubt, as strange as this may seem to some, the force that compelled me on my search for Christ was the swirling, maddening, tumultuous conundrum of sex. Let me explain.

Desire—eros, or erotic desire, to be more specific—kicked in pretty early in my life. I was often overwhelmed by a gnawing hunger and thirst I didn't know how to handle. God bless my parents and my Catholic school teachers—they all tried—but people can't give what they don't have. No one had formed them in the true beauty and splendor of God's plan for erotic desire, so they couldn't form me. I was given the traditional biblical "rules" about sex, and my teachers did their best to instill a fear in me of breaking them, but I was never given the "why" behind the "what" of sexual morality.

Okay, those are the rules I shouldn't break, but what the heck am I supposed to do with this crazy desire inside me? The basic message in the air was that sexual desire itself was "dirty" or "bad" and needed to be repressed or otherwise squelched. To put an image to the experience, it seemed the only thing my "Christian" upbringing had to offer me in my hunger was a starvation diet. Eventually the hunger became so intense that it trumped all fear of breaking the rules. As I wrote in my book *Fill These Hearts*, "A person can starve himself for only so long before the choice becomes clear: either I find something to eat, or . . . I'm gonna die. . . . This is why the culture's 'fast-food gospel'—the promise of immediate gratification through indulgence of desire—inevitably wins large numbers of converts from the 'starvation diet gospel.'"[1]

Of course, it's equally true that a person can eat the fast food for only so long before all the grease and sodium take their toll. Once the pleasure of indulging wears off, bad food, I came to learn, is no less destructive than malnutrition.

Were these the only two options for my hunger: death by starvation or death by food poisoning? Was there any "good food" to be had, food that could actually bring life to my aching soul? I wanted answers. I *needed* answers! If God were real, I figured he must have some kind of plan in giving us such strong sexual desires. So in a college dorm in 1988, I let loose a rather desperate cry of my heart, a ragged prayer that went something like this:

God in heaven, if you exist, you better show me! And you better show me what this whole sex thing is all about and why you gave me all these desires, because they're getting me and everybody I know into a lot of trouble. What is your plan? Do you have a plan? Show me! Please! Show me!

That's when I started studying the Bible, and eventually I encountered Jesus in a living, personal way. He wasn't just an idea to me anymore: I started experiencing the power of his resurrection in my life in dramatic ways, particularly with regard to my sexual brokenness. After years of selfish erotic indulgence, I was experiencing real deliverance and healing from addictive fantasies, attitudes, and behavior.

Soon after my conversion, I became part of an ecumenical community of Protestant and Catholic believers. We had Bible studies together; studied the works of A. W. Tozer, Andrew Murray, and Watchman Nee; prayed together; evangelized together; and enjoyed a committed Christian fellowship. There was a deep fear, however, surrounding sexuality within this group of believers. Grown men and women didn't know how to relate to each other and were largely kept separate. Dating was pretty much forbidden until you got "approval" from the leadership, who, in turn, basically arranged who dated whom without much respect for the freedom of the people involved. Not surprisingly, under the surface of these tightly controlled relationships there was a lot of unaddressed sexual brokenness.

This painfully dysfunctional situation only compelled me all the more to dive into Scripture seeking answers to my questions about God's plan for sex: *There's got to be more than indulgence and repression! There's got to be more than the fast-food diet and the starvation diet. Lord, what is your plan?*

Over a period of about three years of intense, prayerful study of God's Word, I came to see that the Bible takes us on a journey from a wedding in the earthly paradise of Eden to a wedding in the heavenly paradise of the New Jerusalem. I came to see that the Prophets use some boldly erotic images in describing God's love for his people, that the intimate love poetry of the Song of Songs was a window into things of heaven, and that the joining of spouses in "one flesh" was a "profound mystery" that revealed Christ's love for the church (Eph. 5:31–32). In short, the spousal imagery of the Scriptures was bringing my faith to life, shedding light on the entire mystery of our creation, fall, and redemption in Christ. Yes, yes—there *was* more than the starvation diet and the fast-food diet! It's called *the marriage feast of the Lamb*! And Christ didn't come to *repress* our desires; he came to *redeem* our desires—to heal them, to redirect human hunger and thirst toward his eternal banquet of love.

Oh! I was on fire . . .

Expecting an enthusiastic response from the people in my Christian fellowship (and knowing how desperately we all needed help in this regard), I was surprised to be met with blank stares or worse when I tried to explain how the union of man and woman in "one flesh" was like a golden key that unlocked the mysteries of the Bible. Confused but not deterred, I started looking elsewhere for confirmation. Then a fateful meeting with a high school theology teacher changed my life forever. Testing some of my "spousal" readings of the Bible on her, she interrupted, "Oh, you must have read John Paul II's Theology of the Body." "What's that?" I probed. She responded, "Gosh, I thought you'd already read it. What you're saying sounds like his teaching."

It turns out that John Paul II's first major teaching project as the bishop of Rome had been a Bible study on God's plan for man and woman so detailed and comprehensive that it spanned five years. It may well be the most in-depth biblical vision of what it means to be created male and female ever presented in Christian history. When I read it for the first time in 1993, I knew I was holding a new kind of sexual revolution in my hands and that I'd spend the rest of my life studying it and sharing it with the world.

Although I began my work translating John Paul II's rather dense scholarship in a predominantly Catholic context, it didn't take long for it to spread across denominational lines. I have been humbled and honored over the years to be invited to address countless Protestant congregations and events. I agree with Craig Carter's prediction that "Protestants, especially evangelicals, will embrace the Theology of the Body in greater and greater numbers in the years ahead" and in doing so "will be in the position to launch the second sexual revolution" through a compellingly positive "Biblical approach to human sexuality and the family."[2]

I owe a tremendous debt of gratitude to my Protestant brothers and sisters for helping to bring me to Christ and for inspiring me to love God's Word as I do. Translating the Theology of the Body into a language more easily accessible to you—the goal of this book—is a small way of saying thanks.

ONE

OUR BODIES TELL GOD'S STORY

I know some muddle-headed Christians have talked as if Christianity thought that sex or the body were bad in themselves. But they were wrong.

—C. S. Lewis

In the early 1900s, a "respectable" woman wore an average of twenty-five pounds of clothing when she appeared in public. The sight of an ankle could cause scandal. Over the next hundred years the pendulum swung to the other extreme. Today, scantily clad, hyper-eroticized images of the human body have become the cultural wallpaper; and graphic, hard-core pornography has become our main reference point for the "facts of life."

Is it any wonder in our post–sexual revolution world that our deepest, most painful wounds as human beings often center on our sexuality? And by "sexuality" I mean not only what we do

1

with our genitals behind closed doors but also our very sense of ourselves as male and female. We live in a world of chaotic, widespread gender confusion, a world that seems intent on erasing the essential meaning of sexual difference from the individual and collective consciousness.

A Bold, Biblical Response to the Sexual Revolution

All of this has posed an enormous challenge to Christians. How have we responded? Those who began acquiescing to what might be called "the new morality" had to reinterpret the Bible in order to do so, a move that eventually led many believers and denominations to abandon the basic tenets of the Christian faith. On the other hand, Christian leaders who upheld traditional biblical faith and morality often found themselves without a convincing language to engage their own congregations, who were being increasingly influenced and formed by the ethos of the secular culture. The same held true for parents with their children. The silence was deafening. "The Bible says so" and "thou shalt not" weren't enough to prevent people from getting carried away by the tide of so-called sexual liberation.

In the early 1950s, right at the time Hugh Hefner launched *Playboy* magazine, a young Polish priest, philosopher, and theologian named Karol Wojtyla (pronounced "voy-tee-wa") started quietly formulating a fresh, bold, compelling, biblical response to this modern brand of liberation. This was a man steadfast in his commitment to traditional Christian values but also open and attentive to the challenges being raised by the modern world. As a student of contemporary philosophy himself, he understood how modern men and women thought, and he believed he could explain the biblical vision of sex in a way that would ring true in their hearts and minds. From Wojtyla's

2

perspective, the problem with the sexual revolution was not that it overvalued sex but that it failed to see how astoundingly valuable it really is. He was convinced that if he could show the utter beauty and splendor of God's plan for the body and sexuality, it would open the way to *true freedom*—the freedom to love as Christ loves.

Over the next twenty years, he continually refined and deepened his vision via the pulpit, the university classroom, and in countless conversations and counseling sessions with dating, engaged, and married couples. (Wojtyla's open, honest approach with young people—no subject was off-limits if sought honestly—was very similar to that of Francis Schaeffer.) In December 1974, now as archbishop of Krakow, he began putting this bold, biblical vision to paper. On page 1 of his handwritten manuscript, he gave it the title "Theology of the Body."

This was an altogether different kind of Bible study on sex. It was not the all-too-common attempt to scour the Scriptures looking for proof texts on immorality. The goal was to examine key passages from Genesis to Revelation—over fifteen hundred in all—in order to paint a total vision of human love in God's plan. In essence, Wojtyla was saying to the modern world, "Okay, you wanna talk about sex? No problem. But let's *really* talk about it. Let's not stop at the surface. Let's have the courage to enter together into what the Bible calls the 'profound mystery' of our sexuality. If we do, we'll discover something more grand and glorious than we have ever dared to imagine."

This was a vision that had the power to change the world—*if* the world only had a chance to hear it. That chance came when, in October of 1978, this little-known Polish bishop was chosen as the first non-Italian pope in 450 years, taking the name John Paul II. Having only recently completed his Theology of the Body manuscript (it was originally intended as a book to be published in Poland), he decided to make it his first major teaching project as pope, delivering small portions of the text over the course of 129 weekly addresses between September of 1979 and November of 1984.

It took some time, however, for people to grasp the significance of what this in-depth Bible study had given the world. It wasn't until 1999, for example, that his biographer George Weigel described the Theology of the Body to a wide readership as "a kind of *theological time-bomb* set to go off with dramatic consequences, . . . perhaps in the twenty-first century." While John Paul II's vision of the body and of sexual love had barely begun to shape the way Christians engaged their faith, Weigel predicted that when it did, it would "compel a dramatic development of thinking" about virtually every major tenet of the Christian faith.[1]

God, Sex, and the Meaning of Life

What might the human body and sex have to do with the basic tenets of Christianity? There is, in fact, a deep, organic connection between the two. As mentioned above, rejection of the biblical vision of sexuality has led in practice to a rejection of the basic principles of the faith. And here's why: if we are made in the image of God as male and female (see Gen. 1:27), and if joining in "one flesh" is a "profound mystery" that refers to Christ and the church (see Eph. 5:31–32), then our understanding of the body, gender, and sexuality has a direct impact on our understanding of God, Christ, and the church.

As we will see throughout this book, to ask questions about the meaning of the body starts us on an exhilarating journey that—if we stay the course—leads us from the body to the mystery of sexual difference; from sexual difference to the mystery of communion in "one flesh"; from communion in "one flesh" to the mystery of Christ's communion with the church; and from the communion of Christ and the church to the greatest mystery of all: the eternal communion found in God among Father, Son, and Holy Spirit. This is what the tenets of Christian faith are all about.

As we're already seeing, the body is not only *biological*. Since we're made in the image of God as male and female, the body, as we will unfold in some detail, is also *theological*. It tells an astounding divine story. And it does so precisely through the mystery of sexual difference and the call of the two to become "one flesh." This means that when we get the body and sex wrong, we get the divine story wrong as well.

Sex is not just about sex. The way we understand and express our sexuality points to our deepest-held convictions about who we are, who God is, who Jesus is, what the church is (or should be), the meaning of love, the ordering of society, and the mystery of the universe. This means that John Paul II's Theology of the Body (henceforth TOB) is much more than a biblical reflection on sex and married love. Through reflecting on those profound mysteries, we are led by the TOB to "the rediscovery of the meaning of the whole of existence . . . the meaning of life."[2]

Christ teaches that his highest will for our lives is to love as he loves (see John 15:12). One of John Paul II's main insights is that God inscribed this vocation to love as he loves *right in our bodies* by creating us male and female and calling us to become "one flesh" (see Gen. 2:24). Far from being a footnote in the Christian life, the way we understand the body and the sexual relationship "concerns the whole Bible."[3] It plunges us into "the perspective of the whole gospel, of the whole teaching, even more, of the whole mission of Christ."[4]

Christ's mission is to reconcile us to the Father and, through that, to restore the order of love in a world seriously distorted by sin. And the union of the sexes, as always, lies at the basis of the human "order of love." Therefore, what we learn in the TOB is obviously "important with regard to marriage." However, it "is equally essential and *valid for the [understanding] of man* in general: for the fundamental problem of understanding him and for the self-understanding of his being in the world."[5]

Looking for the meaning of life? Looking to understand the fundamental questions of existence? Our bodies tell the story. But we must learn how to "read" that story properly, and this is not easy. A great many obstacles, prejudices, taboos, and fears can derail us as we seek to enter the "profound mystery" of our own embodiment as male and female. Indeed, the temptation to disincarnate our humanity and, even more, to disincarnate the Christian faith is constant and fierce. But ours is an *en-fleshed* faith—*everything* hinges on the incarnation! We must be very careful never to *un-flesh* it. It's the enemy who wants to deny Christ's coming in the flesh (see 1 John 4:2–3).

Spirit and Flesh

When it comes to present-day Christianity, people are used to an emphasis on "spiritual" things. In turn, many Christians are unfamiliar, and sometimes rather uncomfortable, with an emphasis on the physical realm, especially the human body. But this is a false and dangerous split. Spirit has priority over matter, since God, in himself, is pure Spirit. Yet God is the author of the physical world, and in his wisdom, he designed physical realities to convey spiritual mysteries. "There is no good trying to be more spiritual than God," as C. S. Lewis insisted. "God never meant man to be a purely spiritual creature. That is why he uses material things like bread and wine to put the new life into us. We may think this rather crude and unspiritual. God does not. . . . He likes matter. He invented it."[6]

We should like it too. For we are not angels "trapped" in physical bodies. We are *incarnate spirits*; we are a marriage of body and soul, of the physical and the spiritual. Living a "spiritual life" as a Christian *never* means fleeing from or disparaging the physical world. Tragically, many Christians grow up thinking of the physical world (especially their own bodies and sexuality) as the main obstacle to the spiritual life, as if the physical world itself were "bad." Much of this thinking, it seems, comes from a faulty reading of the distinction the apostle Paul makes in his letters between Spirit and flesh (see, e.g., Rom. 8:1–17; Gal. 5:16–26).

In Paul's terminology "the flesh" refers to the whole person (body and soul) cut off from God's "in-spiration"—cut off from God's indwelling Spirit. It refers to a person dominated by vice. And in this sense, as Christ himself asserted, "the flesh counts for nothing" (John 6:63). But the person who opens himself to life "according to the Spirit" does *not* reject his body; it's his body that becomes the very dwelling place of the Spirit. "Do you not know that your bodies are temples of the Holy Spirit, who is in you, whom you have received from God? . . . Therefore honor God with your bodies" (1 Cor. 6:19–20).

We honor God with our bodies precisely by welcoming his Spirit into our entire body-soul personality and allowing the Spirit to guide what we do with our bodies. In this way, even our bodies "pass over" from death to life: "And if the Spirit of him who raised Jesus from the dead is living in you, he who raised Christ from the dead will also give life to your mortal bodies because of his Spirit who lives in you" (Rom. 8:11).

Christianity Does Not Reject the Body

The "spirit-good / body-bad" dualism that often passes for Christianity is actually an ancient gnostic error called "Manichaeism," and it couldn't be further from a biblical perspective. In fact, it's a direct attack on Christianity at its deepest roots. If we're to rediscover God's glorious plan for our sexuality, it will be necessary to contend with some ingrained habits in our way of thinking that stem from Manichaeism. So let's take a closer look.

Mani (or Manichaeus), after whom this heresy is named, condemned the body and all things sexual because he believed the material world was evil. Scripture, however, is clear that everything God created is "very good" (see Gen. 1:31). It's critical to let this point sink in. Unwittingly, we often give evil far more weight than it deserves, as if the devil had created his own "evil world" to battle God's "good world." But the devil is a creature, not a creator. And this means *the devil does not have his own clay*. All he can do is take *God's* clay (which is always very good) and twist it, distort it. That's what evil *is*: the twisting or distortion of good. Redemption, therefore, involves the untwisting of what sin and evil have twisted so we can recover the true good.

In today's world, sin and evil have twisted the meaning of the body and sexuality almost beyond recognition. But the solution is never to blame the body itself; it's never to reject or eschew or flee from our sexuality. That approach is gnostic and Manichaean in its very essence. And if that's our approach, we haven't overcome the devil's lies. We've fallen right into his trap. His fundamental goal is always to split body and soul. Why? Well, there's a fancy word for the separation of body and soul. Perhaps you've heard of it: *death*. That's where Manichaeism, like all heresies, leads.

The true solution to all of the pornographic distortions of the body so prevalent today is not the *rejection* of the body but the *redemption* of the body (see Rom. 8:23): the untwisting of what sin has twisted so we can recover the true glory, splendor, and inestimable value of the body. John Paul II summarized the critical distinction between the Manichaean and Christian approaches to the body as follows: If the Manichaean mentality places an "anti-value" on the body and sex, Christianity teaches that the body and sex "always remain a 'value not sufficiently appreciated.'"[7] In other words, if Manichaeism says "the body is bad," Christianity says "the body is so good that we have yet to fathom it."

We must say this loudly, clearly, and repeatedly until it sinks in and heals our wounds: *Christianity does not reject the body!* As C. S. Lewis insisted, "Christianity is almost the only one of the great religions which thoroughly approves of the body—which believes that matter is good, that God himself once took on a human body, that some kind of body is going to be given to us even in heaven and is going to be an essential part of our happiness."[8]

Of course, it would be an oversight not to acknowledge that, in this life, our bodies are often a source of great unhappiness and sometimes terrible suffering. Genetic defects, disease, sickness, injury, and a great many other maladies and misfortunes—not the least of which is the inevitability of death—can cause us to loathe our bodily existence. But, united to the bodily sufferings and death of Christ, our bodily maladies and misfortunes can become something redemptive—both for us and for others. Suffering, as I once heard it said, can either *break us* or *break us open* to the mystery of Christ. Matthew Lee Anderson expressed the conundrum well: "This is the paradox of the body: The body is a temple, but the temple is in ruins.

The incarnation of Jesus affirms the body's original goodness. The death of Jesus reminds us of its need for redemption. And the resurrection of Jesus gives us hope for its restoration."⁹

Word Made Flesh

Establishing the fundamental *goodness* of the body and the hope of bodily redemption is one thing. But what is it that makes the body a "theology," a study of God?

We cannot see God. As pure Spirit, God is totally beyond our vision. Yet the Bible teaches that the invisible God has made himself visible: "That which was from the beginning, which we have heard, which we have seen with our eyes, which we have looked at and our hands have touched—this we proclaim concerning the Word of life. The life appeared; we have seen it" (1 John 1:1–2).

How did John and the other disciples *see* "that which was from the beginning"? How did they *touch* "the Word of life"? "The Word became flesh. . . . We have seen his glory" (John 1:14). Everything about our faith hinges on the incarnation of the Son of God, on the idea that Christ's flesh—and ours, for it's our flesh he took on—has the ability to reveal God's mystery, to make visible the invisible.

If the phrase "theology of the body" seems odd, perhaps it's because we haven't taken the reality of the incarnation as seriously as Scripture does. There's nothing surprising about looking to the human body as a "study of God" if we believe in Christmas. "Through the fact that the Word of God became flesh, the body entered theology . . . through the main door."¹⁰

"Theology of the body," therefore, is not only the title of a series of talks by John Paul II on sex and marriage. The term "theology of the body" expresses the very *logic* of Christianity.

We must say it again (and again) until it sinks in: *everything* in Christianity hinges on the incarnation of the Son of God.

The Thesis Statement

This brings us to the thesis statement of the TOB, the brush with which John Paul II paints the entire vision. It's an incredibly dense statement, but fear not; we'll spend the rest of the book unfolding it. Here it is: "The body, in fact, and only the body, is capable of making visible what is invisible: the spiritual and divine. It has been created to transfer into the visible reality of the world the mystery hidden from eternity in God, and thus to be a sign of it."[11]

Let's begin with the first sentence. Think of your own experiences as a human being: your body is not just a "shell" in which you dwell. Your body is not just *a* body. Your body is not just *any* body. Your body is *some*body—you! Through the profound unity of your body and your soul, your body *reveals* or "makes visible" the invisible reality of your spiritual soul. The "you" that you are is not just a soul "in" a body. Your body is not something you "have" or "own" alongside yourself. Your body *is* you. If someone broke your jaw in a fit of rage, you wouldn't take him to court for "property damage" but for personal assault. What we do with our bodies, and what is done to our bodies, we do or is done to *ourselves*.

Once again, our bodies make visible what is invisible, the spiritual . . . *and the divine.* Aren't we made in the image of God as male and female (see Gen. 1:27)? This means that the very design of our sexually differentiated bodies reveals something about the mystery of God. The phrase "theology of the body" is just another way of stating the bedrock biblical truth that man and woman image God.

11

The body is not divine, of course. Rather, it's an image or a sign of the divine. A sign points us to a reality beyond itself and, in some way, makes that reality present to us. The divine mystery always remains infinitely "beyond"; it cannot be reduced to its sign. Yet the sign is indispensable in making visible the invisible mystery. Human beings need signs and symbols to communicate. There's no way around it. The same holds true in our relationship with God. God speaks to us in "sign language."

Tragically, after sin, the "body loses its character as a sign"[12]— not objectively, but in our subjective perception of it. In other words, in itself, the body still speaks God's sign language, but we don't know how to read it. We've been blinded to the true meaning and beauty of the body. As a result, we tend to consider the body as merely a physical "thing" entirely separated from the spiritual and the divine realms. Tragically, we can spend our whole lives as Christians stuck in this blindness, never knowing that our bodies are a sign revealing the "mystery hidden in God."

The Divine Mystery

Paul wrote that his mission as an apostle of Jesus Christ was "to make plain to everyone . . . this mystery, which for ages past was kept hidden in God" (Eph. 3:9). What is that "mystery hidden in God," and how can it be "made plain to everyone"?

In a specific sense, Paul is talking about the fact that "the Gentiles are heirs together with Israel" (Eph. 3:6). In a broader sense, the biblical term "mystery" refers to the innermost "secret" of God and to his eternal plan for humanity. These realities are so far beyond anything we can comprehend on our own that all we can really utter is the word "mystery." And yet

God's secret is "knowable"—not based on our ability to decipher some divine puzzle but because God has made it known in Jesus Christ.

What has Jesus made known about the innermost secret of God? Dennis Kinlaw, former president of Asbury College, summarized it remarkably well. Jesus, he writes, gives us a "picture of the life of God as seen 'from the inside.'" And from this perspective "we discover the key for comprehending God: *self-giving love*. . . . Love is his inner life, the divine life, which the three persons of the blessed Trinity co-inherently share."[13]

God is not a tyrant; God is not a slave driver; God is not merely a legislator or lawgiver; and he's certainly not an old man with a white beard waiting to strike us down whenever we fail. God is an eternal exchange of love and bliss. He's an infinite "communion of persons," to use John Paul II's preferred expression. And he created us for one reason: to share his eternal love and bliss with us. This is what makes the gospel *good news*: there is a banquet of love that corresponds to the hungry cry of our hearts, and it is God's free gift to us! He has destined us in Christ "before the creation of the world" (Eph. 1:4) to be part of his family, to share in his love (see Eph. 1:9–14).

Kinlaw states, "Salvation is a gift of the Father through the Son and by the Spirit to bring [us], not just to forgiveness and reconciliation with God, but into participation in the very communion that the three persons of the triune Godhead know [among] themselves."[14]

This is the "mystery hidden for ages past in God" that Paul wanted to "make plain to everyone." How did he do it? In Ephesians 5, Paul reveals that this "mystery" isn't far from us. We needn't climb some high mountain to find it. We needn't cross the sea. It's already as "plain" to us as the bodies God gave us when he created us male and female and called the two to become "one flesh." We need only recover our ability to read God's sign language to see it.

The Bible Tells a Marital Story

Scripture uses many images to help us understand God's love. Each has its own valuable place. But the gift of Christ's body on the cross gives "definitive prominence to the spousal meaning of God's love."[15] In fact, from beginning to end, in the mysteries of our creation, fall, and redemption, the Bible tells a covenant story of marital love.

It begins in Genesis with the marriage of the first man and woman, and it ends in Revelation with the marriage of Christ and the church. And these spousal "bookends" provide the key for understanding all that lies between. Indeed, we can summarize all of Sacred Scripture with five simple yet astounding words: *God wants to marry us.*

> As a young man marries a young woman
> so will your Builder marry you;
> as a bridegroom rejoices over his bride,
> so will your God rejoice over you. (Isa. 62:5)

Your breasts had formed and your hair had grown, yet you were stark naked. Later I passed by, and when I looked at you and saw that you were old enough for love, . . . I gave you my solemn oath and entered into a covenant with you, declares the Sovereign LORD, and you became mine. (Ezek. 16:7–8)

> I will betroth you to me forever;
> I will betroth you in righteousness and justice,
> in love and compassion.
> I will betroth you in faithfulness. (Hosea 2:19–20)

God is inviting each of us, in a unique and unrepeatable way, to an unimagined intimacy with him, akin to the intimacy of spouses in "one flesh." While we may need to work through some discomfort or fear here to reclaim the true sacredness, the true holiness, of the imagery, the scandalous truth is that Scripture describes God's love for his people using boldly erotic images. We are probably more familiar (and more comfortable) describing this love as *agape*—the Greek word for sacrificial, self-giving love. Yet one of the most astounding revelations of Sacred Scripture is that God loves as a bridegroom with all the passion of *eros*—an eros that is also totally agape.

One need only think of the Song of Songs. This unabashed celebration of erotic love is not only a biblical celebration of marital intimacy; it's also an image of how God loves his people, fulfilled in Christ's love for the church. And the Song of Songs is not a footnote in the biblical story. In fact, you'll find it at the very center of your Bible for a reason (if your Bible is 1,000 pages, you'll find the Song of Songs right around page 500). The greatest saints in history have understood this erotic love poetry as an expression of the very essence of biblical faith: not only does God love us, he loves us so utterly that he has wed himself to us forever in Jesus Christ. The Bible calls it the "wedding of the Lamb" (Rev. 19:7).

But there's more. Remember that pithy rhyme we learned as children: "First comes love, then comes marriage, then comes the baby in the baby carriage"? We probably didn't realize that we were actually reciting some profound *theology*: theology *of the body*! Our bodies tell the story that God loves us, wants to marry us, and wants us (the bride) to "conceive" his eternal life within us. And this isn't merely a metaphor. Two thousand years ago, a young Jewish woman gave her yes to God's marriage proposal with such totality, with such fidelity, that she literally conceived eternal life in her womb. This radical yes is why Christians have always honored Mary. She is the perfect model of what it means to be a believer, to be open to Jesus, to receive his divine life. (Guys, I know all this bridal imagery can make us uneasy. Think of it this way: Jesus is the quarterback and we are the wide receivers. Our job is to get ourselves open!)

Climax of the Spousal Analogy

As we unfold the biblical analogy of spousal love, it's very important to understand the bounds within which we're using such language and imagery. Analogies, of course, always indicate, at the same time, both similarity and substantial dissimilarity. Without this recognition, there is a real danger of using human realities to infer too much about divine realities.

"It is obvious that the analogy of . . . human spousal love, cannot offer an adequate and complete understanding of . . . the divine mystery." God's "*mystery* remains *transcendent with respect to this analogy* as with respect to any other analogy." At the same time, however, the spousal analogy allows a certain "penetration" into the very essence of the mystery.[16] And no biblical author reaches more deeply into this essence than the apostle Paul in Ephesians 5.

Quoting directly from Genesis 2:24, Paul states: "For this reason a man will leave his father and mother and be united to his wife, and the two will become one flesh." Then, linking the original marriage with the ultimate marriage, he adds: "This is a profound mystery—but I am talking about Christ and the church" (Eph. 5:31–32). Inspired by the Holy Spirit, Paul employs the intimacy of marital union to reveal not just some aspect of the Christian mystery. Rather, spousal union illuminates the reality of our union with Christ in its entirety, the reality of salvation itself. Martin Luther explains as follows: "[Faith] unites the soul with Christ as a bride is united with her bridegroom. . . . Christ is full of grace, life, and salvation. The soul is full of sins, death, and damnation. Now let faith come between them and sins, death, and damnation will be Christ's while grace, life, and salvation will be the soul's; for if Christ is the bridegroom, he must take upon himself the things which are the bride's and bestow upon her the things which are his."[17]

Could there be a more compelling demonstration of Christ's love than to make himself *one with his bride* even to the point of suffering as his own the death that was hers so that he might offer her his own divine life? For the ancients, immersed as they were in this spousal reading of salvation, it was not uncommon to speak of the "mad eros"[18] revealed on the "marriage bed of the cross."[19] All of this is revealed in Ephesians 5:31–32, which is why John Paul II sees in this passage the "crowning" of all of the themes in Sacred Scripture—the "central reality" of the whole of divine revelation.[20] The mystery spoken of in this passage "is *'great' indeed*," he says. "It is what God . . . wishes above all to transmit to mankind in his Word."[21]

But let's be more specific. How does Genesis 2:24 refer to Christ and the church? Christ, the new Adam, "left" his Father in heaven. He also left the home of his mother on earth. Why? To give up his body for his bride (the church) so that she might enter into holy communion with him. In the breaking of the bread, "Christ is united with his 'body' as the bridegroom with the bride. All this is contained in the Letter to the Ephesians."[22]

Allow me to concretize this glorious truth with a family story. I never met my father-in-law; he died when my wife was a young girl. But I admire him tremendously because of the intuition he had as a new husband. At church the day after his wedding, having consummated his marriage the night before, he was in tears as he came back to the pew after receiving communion. When his new bride inquired, he said, "For the first time in my life I understood the meaning of those words, 'This is my body given for you.'"

Make no mistake: when all of the smoke is cleared and all of the distortions are untwisted, the deepest meaning and purpose of human sexuality is to point us to the "wedding supper of the Lamb" (Rev. 19:9). In other words, God created us male and female right from the beginning to live in a "holy communion" that foreshadows the holy communion of Christ and the church. And this is precisely why questions of marriage and sexuality place us right in the center of "the situation in which *the powers of good and evil fight against each other.*"[23]

The Body and the Spiritual Battle

If God created the body and sexual union to proclaim his own eternal mystery of love, why do we not typically see and experience them in this profound way? For example, when you hear the word "sex," what generally comes to mind? Is it the "profound mystery" of Ephesians 5? Or is it something, shall we say, a little less sacred than that? Remember, it's because of sin that the body loses its character as a sign of the divine mystery.

Ponder this for a moment: if the union of the sexes is the original sign in this world of our call to union with God, and if there is an enemy who wants to separate us from God, where do you think he's going to aim his most poisonous arrows? If we want to know what is most sacred in this world, all we need do is look for what is most violently profaned.

The enemy knows that the body and sex are meant to proclaim the divine mystery. And from his perspective, *this proclamation*

18

must be stifled; men and women *must be kept from recognizing the mystery of God in their bodies*. And this is precisely the blindness that original sin introduced at the serpent's prompting, a blindness responsible for so much brokenness and human misery. The good news is that Christ came preaching the recovery of sight for the blind (see Luke 4:18).

For now, the point to keep in mind is that the battle for man's soul is fought over the truth of his body. It's no coincidence that Paul follows his presentation of the "profound mystery" of the "one flesh" union in Ephesians 5 with the call in Ephesians 6 to put on our armor and take up arms in the cosmic struggle between good and evil. As the source of the family and life itself, the union of the sexes "is placed at the center of the great struggle between good and evil, between life and death, between love and all that is opposed to love."[24] Therefore, if we are to win the spiritual battle, the first thing we must do according to Paul is gird our loins with the truth (see Eph. 6:14). The TOB is a clarion call for all men and women to do just that—to gird our loins with the truth that will set us free to love.

The Foundation of Ethics and Culture

The stakes are incredibly high in the cultural debate about the meaning of sex and marriage. In short, as sex goes, so goes marriage; as marriage goes, so goes the family. And because the family is the fundamental cell of society, as the family goes, so goes the culture. This is why confusion about sexual morality "involves a danger perhaps greater than is generally realized: the danger of confusing the basic and fundamental human tendencies, the main paths of human existence. Such confusion must clearly affect the whole spiritual position of man."[25]

Think how intertwined sex is with the very reality of human existence. You simply would not exist without the sexual union of your parents . . . and their parents . . . and their parents . . . and their parents. Every human being is the end result of thousands upon thousands of indispensable sexual unions. Go back any number of generations in your family tree and remove just one sexual union from your lineage and you would not exist. Nor would anyone else who descended from that union. The world would be a different place.

When we tinker with God's plan for sex, we are tinkering with the cosmic stream of human existence. The human race— its very existence, its proper balance—is literally determined by who is having sex with whom, and in what manner. When sexual union is oriented toward love and life, it builds families and, in turn, cultures that live the truth of love and life. When it is oriented against love and life, sexual behavior breeds death— what we can grimly, yet accurately, describe as a "culture of death."

The Interconnection of Sex and the Whole of Life

A culture of death is a culture that separates body and soul (remember, that's what death *is*). In turn, it cannot recognize the body as a "sign" of anything spiritual, let alone divine. It can't recognize the "profound mystery" of married love and procreation. Sex, instead, gets reduced merely to the pursuit of pleasure.

Sexual pleasure is a great blessing and gift from God, of course. But it's meant to be the fruit of loving as he loves, not an end in itself. When pleasure becomes the main goal of sex, society becomes utilitarian. You're valued if you're useful. And, in this case, you're "useful" if you're sexually stimulating. If you're not, or if you get in the way of my pleasure, you will be ignored, discarded, maybe even exterminated. When pleasure is the main goal of sex, people become the means and babies become the obstacle. So we take our pleasure, and we kill our offspring. This is not some dire prediction of an apocalyptic future. *This is the culture we live in now*: a culture of death.

This is why it "is an illusion to think we can build a true culture of human life if we do not . . . accept and experience sexuality and love and the whole of life according to their true meaning and their close inter-connection."[26] But that will never happen unless we can demonstrate that the biblical sexual ethic is not the prudish list of prohibitions it's so often assumed to be. Rather, it's an invitation to live and embrace the love for which we most deeply yearn.

The Underlying Approach

One of the main reasons the TOB resonates so deeply with people is the philosophical approach that undergirds it. In contrast to more conventional philosophical approaches that begin with *objective* and abstract categories and concepts, John Paul II's philosophical approach begins with the very familiar *subjective* realm of human experience. He believes that if what the Bible teaches is objectively true, then human experience—subjective as it is—should offer confirmation of that truth. Knowing that the Bible's message is in harmony with the most secret desires of the human heart, John Paul II does not need, nor does he attempt, to force assent to his proposals. Rather, he invites men and women to reflect honestly on their own experience of life to see if it confirms his proposals.

Those who have been turned off by judgmental moralizers will find this approach delightfully refreshing. John Paul II imposes nothing and wags a finger at *no one*. He simply reflects lovingly on God's Word and on human experience in order to demonstrate the profound harmony between them. Then, with utmost respect for our freedom, he invites us to embrace our own dignity. It doesn't matter how often we have settled for something less. This is a message of sexual healing and redemption, not condemnation.

With this compassionate and merciful approach—the gospel approach—John Paul II shifts the discussion about sex from *legalism* to *liberty*. The legalist asks, "How far can I go before I break the law?" Instead, John Paul II asks, "What is the truth about sex that *sets me free* to love?" To answer that question, we must ask why God made us male and female in the first place. These are questions that plunge us into the deepest truth of what it means to be human. Indeed, the fundamental fact of human existence is that God created us male and female.

What John Paul II's TOB is primarily after, then, is the full truth of what it means to be human—or, as he puts it, a "total vision of man." To discover this "total vision," we must turn to Christ, the one who alone fully reveals what it means to be human. And so, in the first three chapters of the TOB, John Paul II turns to three key words of Jesus—three appeals Jesus makes—that paint a three-paneled picture of where we've come from (*our origin*), where we are now (*our history*), and where we're headed (*our destiny*):

1. *Christ appeals to the "beginning"*: based on Jesus's discussion with the Pharisees about God's plan for marriage "at the beginning" (see Matt. 19:3–9).
2. *Christ appeals to the human heart*: based on Jesus's words in the Sermon on the Mount regarding adultery committed "in [the] heart" (see Matt. 5:27–28).

22

3. *Christ appeals to the resurrection*: based on Christ's discussion with the Sadducees regarding the resurrection of the body (see Matt. 22:23–33).

In the next two chapters of his TOB, John Paul II reflects on marriage both as a *divine gift* and as a *human sign* of God's love. Only in light of these two dimensions are we capable of understanding the true "language" of sexual love. And that's where the final chapter of the TOB takes us: to a winning explanation of how the Christian sexual ethic flows very naturally from a "total vision" of what it means to be human.

Having set the stage, we're ready to dive into the main themes of our Bible study.

TWO

SEX IN THE GARDEN OF EDEN

This is the body: a witness . . . to Love.
—John Paul II

Over the last few years, I've taken up backpacking with my sons. Venturing off into God's creation for several days, away from everything, with all you need strapped to your back; the smell of the woods; crystal clear streams, waterfalls, and swimming holes; views from the summit after a long climb; cooking breakfast over the fire—I love it! Getting eaten alive by mosquitos; getting soaked to the bone by rain; and having no choice but to plod forward when your back is killing you, your legs want to give out, and each step causes your blisters to scream—I hate it! In fact, the *best* thing about a backpacking trip is getting to the car you left behind five days and fifty miles earlier. So why leave the car in the first place? It's all about the *journey*.

25

The Gospels are filled with stories of Jesus teaching his disciples as they walked. I think that's telling. Jesus came to teach us a *way*. He invites us on a journey with him. Backpacking, for me, in both the joys and the trials, gives visceral, bodily expression to what I experience inwardly on the journey of following Christ.

Following the "Sign" in Search of Christ

It seems we can see something similar in the story of the Magi who came in search of Christ (see Matt. 2:1–12). It's fitting that we sometimes call them "Wise Men," for they had the wisdom of the Spirit to recognize a star in the sky as a sign of Christ. The physical universe itself was "calling" to them to search for the God who had made the universe. And—astonishingly—the God who made the universe had now entered it, being "born of a woman" (Gal. 4:4). Following courageously wherever that star led, facing various dangers and hardships, the Magi stayed the course of their journey and came, as Matthew reports, "to worship him" (Matt. 2:2).

As we observed in the previous chapter, God speaks to us in sign language, revealing himself through the veil of this physical world. Almost everyone has experienced that deep sense of awe and wonder in beholding a starlit night, a radiant sunset, or a beautiful flower. In these moments, whether people realize it or not, the physical universe is calling us on a journey of faith in search of Christ. The beauty of the physical world is a "sign" of ultimate Beauty itself (or, rather, *himself*). The physical world is the "theater of God's glory," to use John Calvin's expression. Or, as Paul tells us, God's invisible qualities can be seen from what he has made (see Rom. 1:20).

And yet there's something more grand than any starlit night, sunset, or flower. There's something at the pinnacle of creation that God designed to speak his sign language more potently, more poignantly, than anything else: *us*. For "God created mankind in his own image, in the image of God he created him; male and female he created them. God blessed them and said to them, 'Be fruitful and increase in number'" (Gen. 1:27–28).

Much like the Magi, as we venture into the content of John Paul II's TOB, we will need the wisdom of the Spirit to grasp the meaning of the body as a "sign" and the courage to follow that sign wherever it leads us. It's a long journey. In fact, in this life it never ends, because on a journey toward infinite mystery, there's always more to discover. And the more we come to discover, the more we come to worship him, as the Magi did. Along the "way" there will be times when your back is killing and your legs want to give out. Keep going! The view from the summit is *stupendous*!

Christ Appeals to the Beginning

When some Pharisees questioned Jesus about the meaning of marriage, Jesus responded, "Haven't you read . . . that at the beginning the Creator 'made them male and female' . . . ?" (Matt. 19:4).

If we need proof of the pertinence of these words today, look no further than the fact that Facebook recently listed over fifty gender options to choose from when filling out a personal profile. And after complaints that terms such as "intersex," "cisgender," "gender fluid," "gender nonconforming," "gender variant," "neutrois," "non-binary," "pangender," "two-spirit," and multiple other variations on these themes were too limiting, the site added a "free-form field" in which people can now "customize" their gender identity. "We recognize that some people face challenges sharing their true gender identity with others," said Facebook's diversity team in a statement, "and this setting gives people the ability to express themselves in an authentic way."[1]

What does it mean—really—to speak of "true gender identity" and to express it "in an authentic way"? According to Christ, the answers can only be found by returning to God's original purpose for making us male and female, before the confusion of sin obscured it. Only by doing so can we save the term "gender" from a world untethered from reality.

The root "gen"—from which we get words such as generous, generate, genesis, genetics, genealogy, progeny, gender, and genitals—means "to produce" or "give birth to." A person's *gen*-der, therefore, is based on the manner in which that person is designed to *gen*-erate new life. Contrary to widespread secular insistence, a person's gender is not a malleable social construct. Rather, a person's gender is determined by the kind of genitals he or she has. While the sexual and feminist revolutions of the twentieth century were right to challenge certain roles conventionally limited to one or the other gender, there are two roles—one belonging only to men and the other only to women—that are irreplaceable and absolutely indispensable for the survival of the human race: fatherhood and motherhood. When we understand the gender-genitals-generation link, we also understand why a de-gendered society is bound to degenerate. Indeed, failing to honor the God-given meaning of gender places the future of the human race in peril.

Inevitably, the question arises in this context about those people born with ambiguous genitalia. While acknowledging that this is indeed a painful reality of our fallen world, we can observe that everyone "belongs from birth to one of the two sexes. This fact is not contradicted by [those rare cases of] hermaphroditism—any more than any other sickness or deformity militates against the fact that there is such a thing as human nature."[2] In other words, the anomaly doesn't alter the norm. The hope for those who suffer with this anomaly, and for all those with gender confusion of any kind, lies not in science to "assign" a new gender but in Christ to restore the original order of our humanity through the gift of redemption.

Whatever number of "gender identities" the modern world may claim exists, Christ's teaching is definitive: "at the beginning the Creator 'made them male and female'" (Matt. 19:4). Then, quoting from Genesis, he adds, "'For this reason a man will leave his father and mother and be united to his wife, and the two will become one flesh.' So they are no longer two, but one flesh. Therefore what God has joined together"—the two genders, through their complementary genitals, for the sake of generation—"let no one separate" (Matt. 19:4–6).

It Was Not This Way from the Beginning

Shocked by Jesus's insistence on the permanence of marriage, the Pharisees retorted, "Why then . . . did Moses command that a man give his wife a certificate of divorce and send her away?" In response, Christ appealed to the beginning yet again: "Moses permitted you to divorce your wives because your hearts were hard. But it was not this way from the beginning" (Matt. 19:7–8).

In effect, Jesus is saying something like this: "You think all the tension, conflict, and heartache in the male-female relationship is normal? This is not normal. This is not the way God created it to be. Something has gone terribly wrong." At the same time—and this is the good news!—Christ is injecting his listeners with hope: hope of restoration, hope of healing, hope of redemption. Christ came to restore creation to the purity of its origins, beginning with the relationship of man and woman.

It's as if we're all driving around town in cars with flat tires. The rubber is shredding off the rims; the rims are getting all dented up; and we just think this is normal. After all, everyone's tires look this way. Jesus is saying to the Pharisees (and to all of us), "In the beginning, they had air in their tires."

So if we want to know the real story our bodies are meant to tell, according to Christ, we have to go back to "the beginning" before sin distorted things. That's the standard. That's the norm. As we take a deeper look at the creation texts, we will probably realize at a new level just how far we are from "the beginning." But do not despair! Christ came into the world not to condemn those with flat tires. He came into the world to reinflate our flat tires. We cannot actually return to the state of innocence; we've left that behind. But by following Christ we can receive God's original plan for our sexuality and live it with Christ's help.

Original Human Experiences

John Paul II takes a refreshing look at the texts of Genesis, examining them with the aim of considering the first man and woman's *experiences* of the body and sexuality. We, of course, do not have any direct experience of the original state of innocence. Nonetheless, an "echo" of the beginning exists within each of us. The original human experiences "are always at the root of every human experience. . . . Indeed, they are so interwoven with the ordinary things of life that we generally do not realize their extraordinary character."[3]

Three experiences in particular seem to define the human person in "the beginning": *solitude*, *unity*, and *nakedness*.

Much ink could be spilled unpacking the dense scholarship of John Paul II's reflections on these experiences (see my much more extensive book *Theology of the Body Explained*).[4] Here I am presenting only a basic sketch. As I do, see if you do not find an echo of these experiences in your own heart.

Original Solitude: The First Discovery of "Personhood"

"The LORD God said, 'It is not good for the man to be alone. I will make a helper suitable for him'" (Gen. 2:18). The most obvious meaning of this "solitude" is that the man is alone without the woman. But John Paul II mines a deeper meaning from this verse. Genesis 2 doesn't even distinguish between male and female until after Adam's "deep sleep." Here Adam represents all of us (*adam* in Hebrew means "man" in the generic sense). Man is "alone" because he is the only bodily creature made in God's image and likeness. In other words, man is "alone" in the visible world as a *person*.

When Adam names the animals, he also discovers his own "name," his own identity. He was looking for a "helper" but didn't find one among the animals (see Gen. 2:20). Adam *differs* from the animals, and "person" is the word we've coined to make the distinction. What does the human *person* have that the animals don't? In a word, the responsibility that comes with freedom. Adam's behavior isn't determined by bodily instinct. He is created from "the dust" like the animals (he is bodily), but he also has the "breath of life" inspiring his body (see Gen. 2:7). An inspired body is not just *a* body but *some*body. A *person* can choose what to do with his or her body. Mere dust cannot. And with this freedom comes responsibility.

In his freedom Adam experiences himself as a *self*. He is more than an "object" in the world; he is also a "subject." He has an

31

"inner world" or an "inner life." It's impossible to speak of the inner life of a squirrel or a chicken. It's precisely this inner life that the words "subject" and "person" capture. Despite some modern propaganda to the contrary, we know intuitively that chickens are not "people too." We owe respect to all of God's creatures, yet no other bodily creature shares the dignity of being created in God's image. As Jesus says, we "are worth more than many sparrows" (Luke 12:7).

Why was Adam endowed with freedom? Because Adam was called to love—and without freedom, love is impossible. In his solitude, Adam realizes that love is his origin, his vocation, and his destiny. He realizes that, unlike the animals, he is invited to enter a covenant of love with God himself. God is a lover with all the passion of a bridegroom who wants to marry us. It's this relationship of love with God that defines Adam's solitude more than anything else. Tasting this love, he also longs with all his being to share this love (covenant) with another person like himself. This is why it is "not good for the man to be alone."

In his solitude, therefore, Adam has already discovered his twofold vocation: love of God and love of neighbor (see Mark 12:29–31). He has also discovered his capacity to negate this vocation. God *invites* Adam to love; he never *forces* him— because forced love is not love at all. Adam can say yes to God's invitation, or he can say no. And this fundamental choice is expressed and realized *in his body*. Solitude—the first discovery of personhood and freedom—is something spiritual, but it is "experienced" bodily, for the "body expresses the person."[5] We can also say that the body expresses the freedom of the person, or at least it's meant to.

To reclaim a terribly abused phrase and restore its authentic meaning, we can say that God is entirely "pro-choice"—in other words, he is entirely "for" our freedom since he gave us the freedom to choose in the first place. But some choices negate our vocation to love. Some choices can *never* bring happiness. We *are* "free," in a sense, to "do whatever we want with our bodies." However, we are not free to determine whether what we do with our bodies is good or evil. As Adam learned, this is a tree (the "tree of the knowledge of good and evil") from which he cannot eat, lest he die (see Gen. 2:16–17). Therefore, human freedom (i.e., choice) is fully realized not by inventing good and evil but by choosing properly between them.

All of these insights are contained in the experience of Adam's solitude. Freedom is given for the sake of love. It's intended to establish communion and bestow life. Cut off from love, self-indulgence masquerades as freedom and leads to rupture and death. What kind of freedom do we want? It's our *choice*.

Original Unity: The Communion of Persons

After Adam named all the animals without finding a person among them, we can imagine his sentiment when God fashioned woman and presented her to him. Adam's cry, "This at last is bone of my bones and flesh of my flesh" (Gen. 2:23 ESV), expresses absolute wonder and fascination.

Notice the bodily focus. Adam is fascinated with *her body* because, as John Paul II points out, this "at last" is a body that expresses a person. All the animals Adam named were bodies but not persons. We lose this in English, but for the Jews, "flesh and bones" signified the whole human being. Hence, woman's creation from one of the man's bones (see Gen. 2:21–22) is a figurative way of expressing that both men and women share the same humanity. Both are persons made in God's image. Both are "alone" in the world in the sense that they are both *different* from the animals (original solitude); both are called to live in a covenant of love. Their sexual desires are not driven by instinct, as with the animals. Since eros was perfectly integrated with agape, they experience sexual desire as the freedom to love in the image of God.

"That is why a man leaves his father and mother and is united to his wife, and they become one flesh" (Gen. 2:24). This experience of *unity* overcomes man's *solitude* in the sense of being alone without the "other." But it affirms everything about human solitude in the sense that man and woman are both persons different from the animals. The human union in "one flesh" is worlds apart from the copulation of animals. What's the big difference? Admittedly, it looks much the same biologically, but human sexual union is not merely a biological reality. It's also a spiritual and a *theological* reality. Becoming "one flesh," therefore, not only refers to the joining of two bodies (as with animals) but corresponds to the communion of persons.

Animals are able to mate, but they're not able to enter "communion." Only *persons* are capable of the "gift of self" that establishes a "*common-union*"—hence the importance of the term "communion of persons" for John Paul II in understanding the meaning of human sexuality. *Human* sexuality differs from *animal* sexuality inasmuch as men and women are made in the divine image and animals are not.

Becoming "one flesh" is a sacramental expression, inasmuch as the body makes visible the invisible mystery of God. That's the most basic meaning of "sacrament" or "sacramentality"— the making visible of the invisible. In the call of man and woman to a "communion of persons," the human body makes visible the invisible mystery of God who himself is an eternal *communion of persons*—the Holy Trinity.

Within the Trinity, the Father eternally "begets" the Son by *giving himself* to and for the Son. In turn, the Son (the "beloved of the Father") eternally receives the love of the Father and eternally gives himself back to the Father. The love they share *is* the Holy Spirit, who "proceeds from the Father and the Son" (Nicene Creed).

Traditionally, theologians have said we image God as individuals through our rational soul. That's certainly true. However, the function of man and woman being made in the image of God is that of mirroring the one who is the model (God), and God is not an eternal "solitude." God is an eternal communion of three persons. This means the human person images God "not only through his own humanity, but also through the communion of persons which man and woman form right from the beginning." And on "all this, right from the beginning, the blessing of fruitfulness descended."[6]

This "blessing of fruitfulness" reveals the mystery of a "third" who proceeds from them both. In this way, authentic sexual love becomes an icon or earthly image of the inner life of the Trinity. Of course, none of this means that God is sexual. The mystery of love and generation in the Trinity is infinitely beyond that of human love and generation. And this means the earthly image pales in comparison to the divine reality. Nonetheless, as Tim Keller points out, "sex is sacred because it is the analogy of the joyous self-giving and pleasure of love within the life of the Trinity."[7] God created us as male and female and called us to life-giving communion precisely to reveal his eternal mystery of love in the temporal dimension.

Original Nakedness: The Key to God's Original Plan

Having discussed the original experiences of *solitude* and *unity*, we are ready to explore the third original experience—*nakedness*.

After the words describing their unity in "one flesh," we read that "Adam and his wife were both naked, and they felt no shame" (Gen. 2:25). Of all the passages regarding our creation, John Paul II says that this one is "precisely the key" for understanding God's original plan for human life. That's a bold assertion. But how can we understand original nakedness when we, having inherited the "fig leaves," have no direct experience of it? We do so only by contrast—by looking at our own experience of shame and flipping it over.

A woman does not feel the need to cover her body when she is alone in the shower. But if a strange man were to burst into the bathroom, she would. Why? John Paul II proposes that "shame" in this sense is a form of self-defense against being treated as an object for sexual use. In the case of this woman, she knows that she is never meant to be treated as a "thing" for someone's selfish pleasure. Experience teaches her that men (because of the lustful desire that resulted from original sin) tend to objectify women's bodies. Therefore, the woman covers her body not because it's "bad" or "shameful" but to protect her own dignity from the stranger's lustful look—a look that fails to respect her God-given dignity as a person.

Take this experience of fear (shame) in the presence of another person, "flip it over," and we arrive at Adam and Eve's experience of nakedness *without* shame. Lust (self-seeking sexual desire) had not yet entered the human heart. Hence, our first parents experienced a total defenselessness in each other's presence because the other's look posed no threat whatsoever to their dignity. They "see and know each other . . . with all the peace of the interior gaze."[8] This "interior gaze" indicates the sight not just of a body but of a body that reveals a personal and spiritual mystery. They saw God's plan of love (theology) inscribed in their naked bodies, and *that is exactly what they desired*—to love as God loves in and through their bodies. And there is no fear (shame) in love. "Perfect love drives out fear" (1 John 4:18).

"Nakedness without shame" is therefore the key for understanding God's plan for our lives—it reveals the original truth of love. Let this point sink in: God gave us eros "in the beginning" to be the very power to express agape. In other words, he gave us sexual desire to be the power to love as he loves—in a free, sincere, and total gift of self. *This is how the original married couple experienced it.* Sexual desire was not felt as a compulsion or instinct for selfish gratification. The experience of lust comes only with the dawn of sin. Lustful sexual desire is a result of what we might call "flat-tire syndrome."

Since the first man and woman were "fully inflated" with God's love, they were entirely free to be a gift to each other. They were *"free with the very freedom of the gift."*[9] Only a person who is free from the compulsion of lust is capable of being a true "gift" to another. The "freedom of the gift," then, is the freedom of the heart to *bless*, which is the freedom from the compulsion to *grasp* and *possess*. It is this freedom that allowed the first couple to be "naked without shame."

As a result of sin, our experience of erotic desire has become terribly distorted. In the midst of these distortions, we can tend to think that there must be something wrong with sex and sexual desire itself (the "body = bad / sex = dirty" mentality stems from this). But the distortions we know so well are *not* at the core of sex. At the core of sex we discover a sign of God's own goodness: "God saw all that he had made, and it was very good" (Gen. 1:31).

According to John Paul II, nakedness without shame demonstrates that the first couple saw what God saw: their own goodness. They *knew* their goodness. They *knew* God's glorious plan of love. They *saw* it inscribed in their bodies, and they *experienced* it in their mutual desire (eros). We lost this glorious vision with the dawn of sin. But don't forget that Jesus came to restore creation to the purity of its origins. This restoration will not be complete until heaven, yet through the gift of redemption we can begin even in this life to reclaim what was lost.

The Spousal Meaning of the Body

Since lust so often holds sway in our fallen world, nakedness is often intertwined with all that is unholy. But, John Paul II says, in the beginning it was nakedness that revealed God's holiness in the visible world. God's holiness is his eternal mystery of self-giving love—the "exchange of love" among Father, Son, and Holy Spirit. Human holiness, in turn, is what enables "man to express himself deeply with his own body . . . precisely through the 'sincere gift' of self."[10]

Because the Trinity lives an eternal exchange of self-giving love, John Paul II insists that we can discover our true selves only by learning how to make a sincere gift of ourselves. In fact, God inscribed this call to self-giving love *right in our bodies*. Think about it: A man's body makes no sense by itself. Nor does a woman's body. But seen in light of each other, sexual difference reveals the unmistakable plan of God that man and woman are meant to be a "gift" to one another in spousal love.

Hence, in their nakedness the first man and woman discovered what John Paul II calls "the spousal meaning of the body." This is one of the most important terms in our study, one we will return to many times. In short, spousal love (we could also say marital, nuptial, or conjugal love) is the love of *total self-donation*. The spousal meaning of the body, therefore, is the body's "*power to express love: precisely that love in which the human person becomes a gift* and—through this gift—fulfills the very meaning of his being and existence."[11]

If you are looking for the meaning of life, according to John Paul II, it's impressed right in your body—in your sexuality! The purpose of life is to love as God loves, and this is what your body as a man or a woman calls you to.

Let's be more specific. A man's body is complete in all of its systems but one. A woman's body is complete in all of its systems but one. And those respective systems—the reproductive systems—function only in union with the other. We can see that man and woman are meant to be a "gift" to one another even at the cellular level. Every cell in a man's body has forty-six chromosomes . . . except for one. Every cell in a woman's body has forty-six chromosomes . . . except for one. The sperm cell and the ovum each have only twenty-three. Man and woman are meant to complete each other; and in the normal course of events, their reciprocal "giving" enables sperm and ovum to meet, and a "third" comes into existence. As John Paul II expresses it, "knowledge" leads to generation: "Adam *knew* Eve his wife, and she conceived" (Gen. 4:1 RSV).

Fatherhood and motherhood crown and reveal the mystery of sexuality. God's first directive in Genesis, "be fruitful" (Gen. 1:28), is not merely an injunction to propagate. It's a call to love in God's image and thus to "fulfill the very meaning of [our] being and existence."[12]

The Fundamental Component of Existence

Marriage and procreation, of course, are not the only ways to "love as God loves." Although they serve as the original model, whenever we make a sincere gift of ourselves to others—through our daily work, acts of generosity and caring, and so on—we express in some way the body's spousal meaning. Married people have the unique privilege of becoming a "gift" to each other through their marital embrace. But what we learn about self-giving love in Genesis applies to everyone, whether married or not.

John Paul II asserts that the spousal meaning of the body is "the fundamental component of human existence in the world."[13] We simply can't properly understand our humanity apart from the call to love as God loves, and God has inextricably linked that call to love with our bodies and the mystery of sexuality. This means that the spousal meaning of the body is "indispensable for knowing who man is and who he ought to be."[14] Who we ought to be are men and women who love in the image of God. Tragically, sin has crippled us in our ability to love according to God's plan "in the beginning." Even so, the spousal meaning of the body remains embedded in the fabric of our humanity as a call to restoration, a call to the "redemption of the body" Christ has won for us. John Paul II observes that "in the whole perspective of his own 'history,' man will not fail to confer a spousal meaning on his own body. Even if this meaning . . . will undergo many distortions, it will always remain [at] the deepest level . . . as a sign of the 'image of God.' Here we also find the road that goes from the mystery of creation to the 'redemption of the body' (see Rom. 8)."[15]

The more we enter into this redemption, the more we rediscover and strengthen the deep bond that exists between the dignity of our humanity and the spousal meaning of our bodies as male and female. And entering more deeply into this redemption is what we aim to do in the next series of reflections.

THREE

THE FALL AND REDEMPTION OF SEX

What if we didn't see passion and desire *as such* as the problem, but rather sought to redirect it? . . . The erotic—even misdirected eros—is a sign of the kinds of animals we are: creatures who *desire* God.

—James K. A. Smith

We began the previous chapter with a reflection on the Magi and the wisdom of the Spirit they were given to recognize the star as a "sign" of something divine. Wise men (and women) are precisely those who know how to read creation's many signs in this way. Speaking of those who did not recognize God's invisible nature in and through the visible things he had made, Paul says, "Although they claimed to be wise, they became fools." They "exchanged the glory of the immortal God for images made to look like a mortal human" (Rom. 1:22–23).

41

Interestingly, Paul says that this exchange of God's glory for human images is the root of sexual lust: "Therefore God gave them over in the sinful desires of their hearts to sexual impurity for the degrading of their bodies with one another. They exchanged the truth about God for a lie, and worshiped and served created things rather than the Creator" (Rom. 1:24–25).

As we saw from our reflections on Genesis, erotic desire in God's original plan enabled man and woman to see their bodies as a sign or icon that pointed to the mystery of God. Eros, in other words, led very naturally and readily from the beauty of the creature to the beauty of the Creator, from delight in the "sign" to worship of the God that their bodies signified. This is what enabled them to be naked without shame (Gen. 2:25): the first man and woman *saw* and *honored* the sacred "iconography" of their bodies.

We all know, of course, that this nakedness without shame did not last very long. The entrance of shame, as we have already seen, indicates a different way of seeing the body; or, rather, it indicates a *failure to see the body as it truly is*: as a sign that points beyond itself to God. When this happens, our desire for Infinite Beauty (eros) gets "stuck" on the body itself. The *icon* becomes an *idol*, and we come to worship the creature rather than the Creator. This, as Paul tells us in Romans 1, is what lust is.

Salvation Begins with Eros

In this chapter, John Paul II will lead us into a deep reflection on the experience of the body and of eros for "historical" men and women. "History," in the sense John Paul II uses the term, begins with original sin and marks a dramatic departure from the experience of "the beginning." But here's the good news: Christ took

42

on a body to redeem our bodies; Christ loved us with a human heart and human desire to redeem our hearts and our desires. As the revered Italian preacher Raniero Cantalamessa plainly stated, Christ has "come to 'save' the world, beginning from the eros which is the dominant force."[1]

What a remarkable assertion! The salvation of the world begins with the salvation of eros. Why does salvation begin here? Because eros, as the dominant force in our lives, has the power to determine "a good or bad lot in the dimension of life as a whole."[2] And precisely because the relationship of man and woman is the deepest foundation of ethics and culture,[3] when eros is misdirected, it leads to the "whole moral disorder that deforms both sexual life and the functioning of *social*, *economic* and even cultural *life*."[4] Christ wants to save each human person and all of humanity at its roots, and *our roots are inextricably linked with eros*.

Because of sin, eros is often experienced as a base human impulse that drags us down toward what is false, twisted, and ugly. Christ comes to restore eros as "the upward impulse of the human spirit toward what is true, good, and beautiful."[5] And we see Christ beginning his work of salvation with eros at the wedding feast of Cana, his first public miracle. Recall that the married couple ran out of wine. Recall also that, throughout Scripture, especially at the Last Supper, wine is a symbol of divine love (agape). Since the dawn of sin, eros has been cut off from agape. Or, to go with the symbolism of Cana, eros has "run out of wine." Christ's first miracle is to restore the wine to eros in superabundance. And he wants us to drink up! "Let anyone who is thirsty come to me and drink" (John 7:37).

Do you know what the goal of the Christian life is from this perspective? It's to get utterly plastered on God's wine. What did the crowd accuse the apostles of on Pentecost when the love of God descended upon them? "You guys are drunk!" (see Acts 2:13–15). And so the gospel invites us to a holy intoxication on God's wine so that our entire humanity—body and soul, sexuality and spirituality—becomes enflamed with divine love. Christ came to set the world on fire (see Luke 12:49)—let's not be afraid to burn!

The Sermon on the Mount

We turn now to the second of the three key words of Christ in our quest for a total vision of man. This time it comes from the Sermon on the Mount: "You have heard that it was said, 'You shall not commit adultery.' But I tell you that anyone who looks at a woman lustfully has already committed adultery with her in his heart" (Matt. 5:27–28).

For the sake of example, Christ speaks directly of the male tendency to objectify women, but the principle applies equally to the ways that women objectify men. It's also part of our fallen world, of course, that some men and women experience lust for their own sex. While homosexuality is a complex and sensitive matter that deserves further treatment than we can offer here, we can at least provide an initial outline of how a biblically faithful theology of the body illuminates this particular issue. First, we can and must affirm all that is true, good, and beautiful about eros in the human heart—including the rightful attraction we should all have toward the goodness of our own sex. However, we must also recognize that eros has been disoriented in each of us by original sin. This means that the way to attain the love we long for isn't simply by submitting to our erotic desires as we now experience them. That's a recipe not for love but for using others for our selfish pleasures. The fact of the matter is that each and every one of us is in need of sexual "re-orientation" according to God's original plan in making us male and female.

The beginning, before sin, is the norm for an authentically biblical understanding of sexuality. Hence, Christ's proclamation—"it was not this way from the beginning" (Matt. 19:8)—is decisive not just for divorce but also for every other way the human heart has veered from God's original plan. The homosexual inclination is just one in a long list of inclinations that stem from our fallen condition. While it's true that these inclinations are inherited with our fallen humanity and not chosen, it's equally true that we can choose whether to foster or to fight these inclinations. We're *all* called to the spiritual battle involved in following Christ; we're *all* called to the purification and healing of our desires. This entails discipline and self-denial, but it's a discipline that's authentically liberating and constructive, not repressive and destructive.

The healing and restoration of God's original plan for eros—that's what Christ's words about lust in the Sermon on the Mount are all about. And they apply equally to everyone, however our fallen inclinations might manifest themselves. Through Christ's appeal to our hearts, we *"must rediscover the lost fullness of [our] humanity and want to regain it."*[6] And there is real power flowing from Christ's words to enable us to do so. It isn't easy. And it doesn't happen overnight. Like Paul, we may carry a particular "thorn" of weakness in our flesh throughout our earthly journey (see 2 Cor. 12:7). Even so, God's grace is sufficient for us to remain faithful to his original "very good" design for our sexuality.

And so we can see that this Theology of the Body is for everybody, regardless of a person's particular struggles. In short, by taking proper account of the beginning, the fall, and the redemption, a biblically sound theology of the body saves us from the strong temptation of normalizing our brokenness, as if God made us that way. It's okay that we're broken. Everyone is. God loves us right there and comes to meet us right there. But it's not okay to call our brokenness "health." So long as we do, we remain closed to God's remedy, like a sick man who sees no need for a doctor because he refuses to admit that he's ill.

Lord, as we continue our study of your saving words, open our hearts to your healing power!

Looking with Lust

When Christ speaks of "looking with lust," he's not saying that a mere glance or momentary thought makes us guilty of adultery in our hearts. As fallen human beings, we will always be able to sense the pull of lust in our hearts and in our bodies. This doesn't mean we have sinned. It's what we do when we experience the pull of lust that matters. Do we seek God's help in resisting it, or do we indulge it? When we indulge it—that is, when we actively choose "in our hearts" to treat another person as merely an object for our own gratification—we seriously violate that person's dignity and our own. We're meant to be loved "for our own sakes," never used as an object for someone else's sake. The opposite of love in this case is not hatred; rather, the opposite of love is to *use* someone as a means to our own selfish ends.

Furthermore, it's significant that Christ refers to looking lustfully at "a woman." He doesn't restrict his words to someone other than a spouse. Hence, John Paul II concludes that a man commits adultery in the heart not only by looking lustfully at a woman he is not married to "but *precisely because he looks in this way at a woman. Even* if he were to look in this way at . . . his wife, he would commit the same adultery 'in the heart.'"[7] Exuberant passion and unbridled joy is a wonderful thing in the marriage bed. But treating a spouse merely as an object for one's selfish indulgence is never an act of love.

Few Christian men understand this crucial point. The books and programs that have flooded the Christian market to help us in our "pornified" culture rarely get this either. The main goal of these programs is to help husbands direct their sexual desires toward their wives—a good first step, of course. But rarely, if ever, do these programs invite men to examine *what kind of desires* they're directing toward their wives. I recall reviewing one such program that, in attempting to relieve husbands of the guilt they sometimes feel for the sexual demands they make on their wives, suggested men should feel no more pang of conscience in this regard than they do in wanting to eat a cheeseburger. While a certain comparison can be made between hunger and sexual desire, have we noticed that this analogy reduces the wife to a piece of meat? If a man approaches his wife as an object of consumption, it's not love at work, it's lust.

I don't want to harp on us men too much here. Women's drives have also become deeply disordered by original sin, and this wreaks havoc in the lives of men. Still, I would agree with John Paul II that, because of their particular biblical calling to image Christ as the bridegroom, men have a "special responsibility" to restore the balance of love in the male-female relationship. It's "as if it depended more on him whether the balance is kept or violated or even—if it has already been violated—reestablished."[8] A critical part of this reestablishment is for spouses to reexamine the motives with which they approach one another for sex.

As I've held out this challenge over the years, I've sometimes been challenged in return by men who appeal to various Bible verses that seem to justify a different approach. But if we want to be honest about Paul's teaching on submission (see Eph. 5:22–23) and the marital duty (1 Cor. 7:3–5), then we must recognize that our marital duty—as Paul states quite clearly—is to love our wives "just as Christ loved the church" (Eph. 5:25). Submitting ourselves to that means there is no justification for treating our wives as objects. Rather, as Paul says to the Thessalonians, "It is God's will . . . that each of you should learn how to control his own body [or live with his own wife] in a way that is holy and honorable, not in passionate lust like the pagans, who do not know God" (1 Thess. 4:3–5).

This is not to say that marital intercourse is not to be passionate. But the passion of lust is one thing, and the passion of imaging and expressing divine love is another. The former is like an untrained person banging recklessly on a piano, making meaningless noise. The latter is like a professional musician who sits at the piano and makes music that lifts our souls to the heavens. Which kind of passion do we prefer? The former takes zero discipline. The latter takes a lifetime of it. Relatively few are called to be professional musicians, but everyone is called to learn how to love divinely.

This is what the apostle Paul calls us to in his letters, and this is what Christ calls us to in his words about lust in the Sermon on the Mount. These words show us "how deep down it is necessary to go, how the innermost recesses of the human heart must be thoroughly revealed, so that this heart might become a place in which the law [of love] is 'fulfilled.'"[9]

Not even the holiest of spouses live the "law of love" perfectly in this regard, but it's critical that we commit ourselves to the journey of allowing God's mercy and grace to transform our hearts. Otherwise, "making love" amounts to little more than "making lust," and this wounds both husbands and wives terribly. Perhaps up to this point you have considered marriage a "legitimate" outlet for lust rather than a path of restoring sexual desire according to God's original plan. If so, maybe Christ is inviting you to allow the light of the gospel to penetrate and illuminate your sexuality in new ways. Be not afraid!

Words of Salvation, Not Condemnation

Christ's words about lust are challenging, even severe. Should we fear the severity of these words or rather have confidence in their power to save us? These words have power to save us because the one who speaks them is the "Lamb of God, who takes away the sin of the world" (John 1:29). Most people see in Christ's words only a condemnation. Do we forget that Christ came into the world not to condemn but to save (see John 3:17)?

Christ's words about lust call us to "enter our full image."[10] As part of the heritage of original sin, lust obscures in each of us God's original, beautiful plan for sexual love—but it has *not* snuffed out God's plan altogether. John Paul II insists that the heritage of our hearts is *deeper* than lust; and if we're honest with ourselves, we still desire what's deeper. If the human heart is a deep well, it's true that murky waters abound. But if we press through the mud and the mire, at the bottom of the well we find a spring that, when activated, gradually fills the well to overflowing with pure, living water. This spring is the "deeper heritage" of our hearts. Christ's words reactivate that deeper heritage, giving it real power in our lives.[11]

This means that we needn't walk through life merely coping with our lusts and disorders. Christ didn't die on a cross and rise from the dead to give us a program of "sin management," to use Dallas Willard's expression.[12] Christ died on a cross and rose from the dead to save us from sin so that we, too, could live a new life (see Rom. 6:4). Again, we need to stress that this "new life" will come to fulfillment only in the resurrection at the end of time; but it's also true that Christ's resurrection is already at work in us. Here and now we can begin to experience the redemption of eros, the transformation of our hearts. But we must earnestly commit ourselves to the journey. As Willard also notes, grace is not opposed to effort, only earning.[13] This is a journey full of peaks and valleys, and we're sure to experience victories and setbacks. But it's a journey that *can* be undertaken. God's grace is enough for us!

Questioning God's Gift

To understand more clearly what the redemption of our sexuality entails, we must first examine how and why we fell from God's original plan. So, once again, John Paul II takes us back to Genesis, this time to examine the nature of the original sin and the entrance of the fig leaves.

He describes original sin as "the questioning of the gift." Allow me to explain. The deepest yearning of the human heart is to be "like God" by sharing in his life and love. Right from the beginning, God had granted man and woman a sharing in his own life and love as a totally free gift. Using the spousal image, God *initiated* the gift of himself as "bridegroom," and man (male and female) opened to *receive* the gift as "bride." In turn, man and woman were able to re-image this same "exchange of love" through their own marital self-giving and unity.

In order to retain this divine likeness and remain in his love, God had asked only that they not eat from "the tree of the knowledge of good and evil." If they did eat of it, they would cut themselves off from the source of life and love. In other words, they would die (see Gen. 2:16–17).

Sounds simple enough. So where did it all go wrong? Satan's no dummy. He knows that God created the union of the sexes as a sharing in divine life, and his goal is to keep us from this. So he aims his attack at *"the very heart of that unity that had, from the 'beginning,' been formed by man and woman*, created and called to become 'one flesh.'"[14]

Having approached the woman—the one who represents us all as "bride" in our *receptivity* to God's gift—the serpent insists, "You will not surely die [if you eat from the forbidden tree]. . . . For God knows that when you eat of it your eyes will be opened, and you will be like God, knowing good and evil" (Gen. 3:4–5). We might read the serpent's temptation like this: "God doesn't love you. He's not looking out for you. He's a tyrant, a slave driver who wants to keep you from what you really want. That's why he told you not to eat from that tree. If you want life and happiness, if you want to be 'like God,' then you have to reach out and *take* it for yourself, because God sure won't give it to you."

Herein lies the *questioning*—and, ultimately, the denial—of God's gift. In the moment they reject their *receptivity* before God and *grasp* at their own "happiness," they turn their backs on God's love, on God's gift. In a way, they cast God's love out of their hearts. "Then the eyes of both of them were opened, and they realized they were naked; so they sewed fig leaves together and made coverings for themselves" (Gen. 3:7).

The tendency to "grasp" seems built into our fallen nature. We can observe it even in little children. I remember when my oldest son was five years old and asked me for a cookie. Before I could even get the cookie out of the box to present it to him as a gift, what did he do? He *grasped* at it. So, taking advantage of this teaching moment, I said to him, "Hold on, you're denying the gift. Your Papa loves you. I want to *give* this cookie to you

51

as a gift. If you believed in the gift, all you would need to do is hold your hands out in confidence and *receive* the cookie as a gift." This is the problem with us all. We do not trust enough in our Father's love, so we grasp at the "cookie."

The Second Discovery of Sex

God said that if Adam and Eve ate from the tree, they would die. They didn't immediately keel over dead, but they did die spiritually. In the act of creation, God had *in-spired* their bodies with his own life and love (see Gen. 2:7). Now their bodies *ex-spired* ("breathed out") God's Spirit. This is the precise moment they "ran out of wine," the precise moment eros "ran out" of agape (divine love).

At this point, a basic principle kicked in: *you can't give what you don't have*. The purpose of the sexual relationship is to share divine love, but they no longer had it to share. What was left? Lust. Having "denied the gift" in their relationship with God, they no longer experienced sexual desire as the power to be a gift to one another. Instead, they desired to *grasp* and *possess* one another for their own gratification. With the dawn of lust, the "*relationship of the gift changes into a relationship of appropriation*."[15] To "appropriate" in this sense means "to take hold of" with the desire to *use*.

John Paul II calls this "the second discovery of sex," and it differs radically from the first.[16] In the first discovery of sex, Adam and Eve experienced total peace and tranquility. Now they immediately feel threatened by the other's "look." Nakedness originally revealed their Godlike dignity. Now they instinctively hide.

Shame, therefore, has a double meaning. It indicates that they have lost sight of the spousal meaning of their bodies (God's plan of love stamped in their sexuality), but it also indicates an inherent need to *protect* the spousal meaning of the body from the degradation of lust. As John Paul II insightfully expresses it, lust "tramples on the ruins" of the spousal meaning of the body and aims to directly satisfy only the "sexual need" of the body.[17] It seeks "the sensation of sexuality" apart from a true gift of self and a true communion of persons. Lust, in fact, shatters their communion.

Lust is often thought of as some benefit to the sexual relationship, or it's conceived of as an *increase* or *intensification* of sexual desire. In reality, lust is a *reduction* of the original fullness God intended for erotic desire. We don't get "more" when we lust; we get much less. The joy of erotic love in God's plan is meant to be a foretaste of the bliss and happiness of heaven. But if eros is meant to lead us to an infinite banquet of love and satisfaction, lust reduces eros to a craving for fast food—immediate gratification that may taste good going down but ultimately leaves us feeling poisoned and used. Indulgence of lust can't possibly reach us where we yearn to be reached, where the "ache" continues to gnaw at us, where the cry of the heart remains as haunting as ever.

Why would we ever choose the fast food over the divine banquet? Because we've "denied the gift." We don't really believe God wants to satisfy our desires. That's the original sin: we "exchanged the truth about God for a lie" (Rom. 1:25) and came to believe that God was holding out on us.

We're created for eternal joy—wired for it. We want infinite pleasure because we're made for God. But when we believe God is holding out on us, we come to believe that the satisfaction of our hunger (eros) is totally up to us, that God's not going to come through for us. Fast food becomes our God substitute, our momentary, fleeting "satisfaction." Shame, in turn, is the result of a deep, interior awareness that something is dread-fully amiss.

"I was afraid because I was naked; so I hid" (Gen. 3:10). From this moment on, shame will cause "a fundamental disquiet in the whole of human existence."[18] Shame, in fact, touches man and woman at their "deepest level and seems to shake the very foundations of their existence."[19] In a way, by covering their bodies with fig leaves (precisely those parts of their bodies that distinguish them and call them to unite), man and woman blame their bodies for lust. But such an approach is quite literally a cover-up—almost an excuse not to face the deep disorder of their hearts.

As Jesus stresses in the Sermon on the Mount, lust is first and foremost a problem of the heart, not of the body. Until we address the disordered desires of our hearts, we will never be able to live as the men and women God created us to be. Lust can affect the male and female personalities differently, but the hearts of both men and women have become battlefields between love and lust.

Christian Ethos: Morality "from the Heart"

Conforming our behavior to an external norm is not enough. We all know it is possible to follow "the rules" without ever attaining holiness (that is, without a heart "in-spired" by God's love). This kind of rigid, lifeless, self-justifying conformity to rules is called legalism or moralism. In the Sermon on the Mount, Christ calls us to something *very* different. He calls us to a "living morality" that flows from the heart.

Jesus sets the stage for this "new" morality when he says, "Unless your righteousness surpasses that of the Pharisees and the teachers of the law, you will certainly not enter the kingdom of heaven" (Matt. 5:20). What could these words have sounded like to the Jews who heard them? The Pharisees and teachers of the law were considered the most righteous of all. But for many of them, at least the ones Jesus singled out, it was all external. They conformed to the ethic, but their "ethos" remained skewed.

An "ethic" is an external norm or rule—"do this / don't do that." "Ethos" refers to a person's inner world of values—what attracts and repulses that person deep in the heart. In the Sermon on the Mount, Christ is not only confirming God's ethical code. He is also proclaiming the true *ethos* of God's commandments— what they call us to *internally*. In effect Christ says, "You've heard the ethic not to commit adultery, but the problem is that you *desire* to commit adultery. Your *ethos* is flawed because you're filled with lust."

It seems almost cruel. Knowing that we are filled with lust, Jesus says, "Don't lust." Great! So what are we supposed to do? Christ holds out a standard that he knows we cannot meet. It seems hopeless—*unless* . . . unless it were possible to experience some kind of redemption or transformation of our desires. This is precisely where the gospel becomes *good news*. As John Paul II repeatedly stresses, the "new ethos" that Christ proclaims in the Sermon on the Mount is not only given to us as a task. It is also given as a gift. We are not left to our own flaws, weaknesses, and sinfulness. In the Sermon on the Mount, Christ speaks a word of power that gives new form to our desires if we but open to receive it deep in the soil of our souls.

"Christian ethos is characterized by *a transformation of the human person's conscience and attitudes . . . such as to express and realize the value of the body and sex* according to the Creator's original plan."[20] What good news! What hope! What joy! We are not *bound* by lust. The new dimension of *ethos* is always connected with the heart's liberation from lust. As we are gradually loosed from the chains of lust, we are freed to love according to God's original plan. This is a living and life-giving morality through which we realize the very meaning of our humanity.

Freedom from the Law

Most people look at Christian morality—especially sexual morality—as an oppressive list of rules to follow. How far this (mis)understanding is from the "living morality" proclaimed by Christ! The gospel doesn't give us more rules to follow. The gospel is meant to *change our hearts* so that we no longer need the rules. To the degree that we experience this change of heart, we experience what the Bible calls "freedom from the law" (see Rom. 7; Gal. 5)—not freedom to break the law; freedom to *fulfill* it.

Here's an example of what freedom from the law looks like: Do you have any desire to murder your best friend? This may seem like an odd question, but it actually demonstrates the point. Assuming you do not, then you do not need the commandment "Thou shalt not murder thy best friend," because you have no desire to break it. To this extent you are "free from the law." In other words, you do not experience this law ("Thou shalt not murder thy best friend") as an imposition, because your heart already conforms to it.

Before sin, the human heart conformed totally to God's will. For example, the first married couple did not need a law forbidding adultery. They had no desire to commit adultery (and not only because there was no one else around). Only with "flat-tire syndrome" do we experience a rupture between our desires and God's will for us. Here is where the law serves its essential purpose. It is given to convict us of sin, as Paul says (see Rom. 7:7). However, when Christ says, "You have heard the commandment . . . but I tell you . . ." he indicates that we need something more than mere precepts can offer.

The Old Testament law is good and just, but it does not of itself give the grace of the Holy Spirit to fulfill it. In other words, it convicts us of having "run out of wine," but it doesn't provide new wine. The law of the gospel, however, reforms the heart and restores the wine in superabundance. To the degree that we are "drunk" on this "new wine," we no longer need the law, because we no longer desire to break it; we are "free from the law."

Here's a question we can ask ourselves to determine where our hearts still need to be liberated: What laws do we still need? What laws feel like a burden or imposition? Perhaps the problem is not with the law but with our own "hardness of heart." If this is where we find ourselves, the solution is not to toss out the law. The solution is to surrender our disordered desires to Christ and let him transform them.

Trying to follow all the rules without drinking deeply of the "new wine" is futile. Those who do will either become self-righteous hypocrites or abandon God's law for a rationalized, watered-down version of the gospel. Either way, it's a "gospel" without the good news; it's Christianity without Christ. Both the self-righteous and the lawless have yet to "pass over" from the bondage of the ethical code to the freedom of the "new ethos"—the freedom of redemption.

Such freedom liberates us not from the *external* constraint that calls us to the good but from the *internal* constraint that hinders our choice of the good. When we *desire* what is true, good, and beautiful, then we are free indeed—free to love and free to bless, which is freedom from the compulsion to *grasp* and *possess*. Those who toss out the law in order to indulge their lusts may imagine themselves free, but like an alcoholic who cannot say no to the bottle, a person who cannot say no to lust is *enslaved*. "It is for freedom that Christ has set us free. Stand firm, then, and do not let yourselves be burdened again by a yoke of slavery" (Gal. 5:1).

The Grace of Creation Becomes the Grace of Redemption

Living in this freedom involves a difficult, uncertain journey as long as we're on earth, but it's made possible by grace, which enables us to possess the full freedom of the children of God (see Rom. 8:21). We are not justified by the law. We are "justified freely by his grace through the redemption that came by Christ Jesus" (Rom. 3:24).

It is this grace that enables men and women to be transformed by the renewal of their minds and offer their bodies as living sacrifices for one another (see Rom. 12:1–2). In the beginning, man and woman were infused with grace; they were drunk on God's wine. When they doubted God's love and "denied the gift," they fell from grace and "ran out of wine." If this is the source of the problem, what is the first step toward a solution? Faith. If original sin is our denial of God's gift, "*faith*, in its deepest essence, is *the openness* of the human heart to the gift: *to God's self-communication in the Holy Spirit*."[21]

In the Sermon on the Mount, when Christ calls us to overcome lust, his words bear witness that the original grace of creation has become for each of us the grace of redemption.[22] The Son of God took on flesh and died on a cross so that our sinful humanity might be put to death. He rose from the dead to "re-create" our humanity. He ascended into heaven with his glorified body to "in-spire" our bodies once again with God's life and love.

Through this gift of our redemption, Christ breathes back into our flesh that same Spirit (grace) that "ex-pired" from our bodies when we denied the gift (see John 20:22). Through this gift of our redemption, he pours the wine of agape back into our eros.

Repent and Believe in the Good News

Jesus's whole life bears witness to the truth that we find so hard to believe: God loves us; he is unequivocally *for* us, not against us. We say, of course, that we believe in God's love: "Jesus loves me this I know / For the Bible tells me so." But the litmus test of our belief in his love is the posture in which we stand before God in our desire. Are we *grasping* at the cookie, or are we *open, receptive*, and *waiting patiently* for God's gift?

In response to that original "denial of the gift" through which all sin entered the world, Christ's life proclaims, "You don't believe God loves you? Let me show you how much God loves you. You don't believe that God is 'gift'? This is my body *given* for you (see Luke 22:19). You think God wants to keep you from life? I will offer myself so that my life's blood can give you life to the full (see John 10:10). You thought God was a tyrant, a slave driver? I will take the form of a slave (see Phil. 2:7); I will let you 'lord it over' me to demonstrate that God has no desire to 'lord it over' you (see Matt. 20:28). You thought God would whip your back if you gave him the chance? I will let you whip my back to demonstrate that God has no desire to whip yours. I have not come to condemn you but to save you (see John 3:17). I have not come to enslave you but to set you free (see Gal. 5:1). Stop persisting in your unbelief. Repent and believe in the good news (see Mark 1:15)."

"God's love has been poured out into our hearts through the Holy Spirit, who has been given to us" (Rom. 5:5). As we open ourselves to this gift, as we come to "know and rely on the love God has for us" (1 John 4:16), the grace of redemption begins to restore our true humanity, to enliven our hearts with God's own goodness. To the degree that we allow this grace to inform and *transform* us, the Holy Spirit impregnates our sexual desires "with everything that is noble and beautiful," with "the supreme value which is love."[23]

Life in the Spirit and the Redemption of the Body

In the apostle Paul's terminology, living the life of grace is synonymous with living "according to the Spirit." He contrasts this, as we observed earlier, with living "according to the flesh." "So I say, walk by the Spirit, and you will not gratify the desires of the flesh. For the flesh desires what is contrary to the Spirit, and the Spirit what is contrary to the flesh" (Gal. 5:16–17).

Recall from what we discussed in chapter 1 that this does *not* mean, as many Christians have tragically concluded, that Paul condemns the body or thinks of it as an inherent obstacle to living a "spiritual" life. As we have been learning throughout our study of God's Word, the body is the specific vehicle of the spiritual life. The person who lives "according to the Spirit" does *not* reject his body but opens his whole body-soul personality to divine *in-spiration*.

With great hope, John Paul II proclaims that as much as lust enslaves us by disordering our passions, "life according to the Spirit" frees us all the more to be a gift to others. As much as lust blinds us to the truth of God's plan for the body, "life according to the Spirit" opens our eyes all the more to the body's spousal meaning. So, to the degree that we open ourselves to "life in the Spirit," we also experience the "redemption of our bodies" (Rom. 8:23).

Paul writes passionately about the redemption of the body in his letter to the Romans, saying that we "groan inwardly" and "wait eagerly" for it (Rom. 8:23). While it's true that we await its fulfillment in heaven, the "redemption of the body" is also already at work in us. This means that as we allow our lusts to be "crucified with Christ" (see Gal. 2:20), we can progressively rediscover that original "spousal meaning of the body" and live it. John Paul II believes that this liberation from lust, and the freedom that it affords, is, in fact, the condition for living all of life together in the truth.[24]

Purity Is Not Prudishness

To the degree that we live out the redemption of our bodies, we understand that sexual purity is not a matter of annihilating or repressing sexual attraction and desire. Mature purity "consists in quickness to affirm the value of the person in every situation, and in raising [sexual reactions] to the personal level."[25] In the Sermon on the Mount, Christ is not simply saying "don't look." Rather, Jesus's words are "an invitation to a pure way of looking at others, capable of respecting the spousal meaning of the body."[26]

Obviously, if a person needs to turn away in order to avoid lusting, then by all means "don't look." Turning away is often a necessary first step, but such an approach could be described as a "negative" purity. As we grow in virtue, we come to experience "positive" or "mature" purity. In mature purity we enjoy the fruits of the victory won over lust. We enjoy the "efficacy of the gift of the Holy Spirit," who restores to our experience of the body "all *its simplicity, its lucid clarity,* and also *its interior joy.*"[27] Practically everyone begins the journey toward mature purity on the "negative" side. Unfortunately, many people stagnate at this stage, thinking it's all they can expect. Keep going. There's more. Much more!

Needless to say, I am far from being a perfect man; following Christ is a daily challenge, and I've fallen in more ways than I'd like to admit. At the same time, in the midst of the struggle, I can attest to the fact that as we appropriate the gift of redemption in our lives, lust loses sway in our hearts. We come not only to understand but also to *see* and *experience* the body as a "theology," a sign of God's own mystery. "Blessed are the pure in heart, for they will see God" (Matt. 5:8). If we understand what Christ is holding out to us here, we can add, "Blessed are the pure in heart, for they will see God's mystery revealed through the body."

Christian purity is not prudishness. It does *not* reject the body. "Purity is the glory of the human body before God. It is the glory of God in the human body, through which masculinity and femininity are manifested."[28] Purity in its fullness will be restored only in heaven. Yet even now purity of heart enables us to see the body as a temple of the Holy Spirit and a manifestation of divine beauty.

The Christian who denies that this kind of purity is possible will either justify his (or her) lusts or remain locked in the rule-obsessed religiosity of the Pharisees. The Pharisees were "constantly stumbling into passersby," writes Alexander Men, the famous biblical scholar and Russian Orthodox priest. "They were afraid to lift their eyes lest they should accidentally look upon a woman. They were called in jest *Khitsay*, 'don't-hit-your-head.' It is natural that Christ's freedom should have irritated and frightened such people; they saw in it temptation and threat to their good morals."[29]

And this, sadly, is how many people view the gospel freedom held out to us in the TOB. Many "religious" people, for example, find themselves scandalized by John Paul II's decision to have several of the loincloths removed from the figures in the Sistine Chapel (loincloths that previous clerics had ordered to be painted over Michelangelo's original nudes). And he did this in the name of Christian purity! During the homily dedicating the restored frescos, John Paul II proclaimed the Sistine Chapel *"the sanctuary of the theology of the human body."* He added, "It seems that Michelangelo, in his own way, allowed himself to be guided by the evocative words of the Book of Genesis which . . . reveals: 'The man and his wife were both naked, yet felt no shame' (Gen. 2:25)."[30]

What, then, is the difference between pornography and a proper artistic portrayal of nakedness? The difference lies in the intention of the artist. Pornographic portrayals of the body raise objection "not because of their object, because in itself the human body always has its own inalienable dignity—but because of the quality or way of its artistic reproduction."[31] The pornographer seeks specifically to arouse lust in the viewer, while the true artist (such as Michelangelo) helps us see "the whole personal mystery of man." Proper portrayals of the naked body can teach us "the spousal meaning of the body which corresponds to, and provides the measure for 'purity of heart.'"[32] Those who experience mature purity understand the naked body for what it is—the revelation of God's plan of love.

The Interpretation of Suspicion

Doubters respond, "Impossible! The naked body will always arouse lust." For the person dominated by lust, this is true. But "of which man are we speaking? Of man *dominated* by lust or of man *redeemed by Christ*? This is what is at stake: the *reality* of Christ's redemption. *Christ has redeemed us!* This means he has given us the possibility of realizing the *entire truth* of our being; he has set our freedom free from the *domination* of lust."[33]

We cannot simply equate nakedness with immodesty and lust. Immodesty is certainly present "when nakedness plays a negative role with regard to the value of the person, when its aim is to arouse [lust]." But "this is not inevitable."[34] If we think a "lustful look" is the only way a person *can* look at the human body, then we subscribe to what John Paul II calls "the interpretation of suspicion." Those who live by suspicion remain so locked in their own lusts that they project the same bondage on everyone else. They cannot imagine any way to think about the human body and the sexual relationship other than through the prism of lust.

When we hold the human heart in a state of continual and irreversible suspicion because of lust, we condemn ourselves to a hopeless, loveless existence. We condemn ourselves to following the rules (*ethics*) without a change of heart (*ethos*). Eventually, we abandon God's law because we simply cannot keep it. This kind of permanent suspicion effectively cuts us off from the *power* of the gospel.

As the apostle Paul warns us, we must avoid the trap of "having a form of godliness but denying its power" (2 Tim. 3:5). "Redemption is a truth, a reality, in the name of which man must feel called, and 'called with effectiveness.'"[35] The death and resurrection of Christ is truly *effective*. It can change our lives, our attitudes, our hearts, and—yes—our sexual desires. To think otherwise is to *empty the cross of its power* (see 1 Cor. 1:17).

Much is at stake. "The meaning of life is the antithesis of the [interpretation] 'of suspicion.'" This interpretation "is very different, *it is radically different* from the one we discover *in Christ's words* in the Sermon on the Mount. These words bring to light . . . another vision of man's possibilities."[36] Unless we tap into this "other vision of man's possibilities," we will find it impossible to love as Christ loves; we will remain cut off from the meaning of life.

Growing in Mature Purity

So how do we tap into this "other vision of man's possibilities"? How do we progress from negative purity to positive? We must begin by devoting ourselves to "a progressive education in self-control of the will, of sentiments, of emotions, which must be developed from the simplest gestures, in which it is relatively easy to put the inner decision into practice."[37] For example, what are your eating habits? If you cannot say no to a potato chip, how are you going to say no to indulging in lust? The biblical practice of fasting is a wonderful way to grow in mastery of our passions. If this is not already part of your life, start with a simple sacrifice that's relatively easy to put into practice. As you continue exercising this "muscle," you will find your strength increasing. What once felt impossible gradually becomes possible.

The muscle analogy, however, is only half right. Growing in purity certainly demands human effort, but we are also aided by supernatural grace. Here it's crucial to distinguish between indulgence, repression, and redemption. When lust flares up, most people think they have only two choices: indulge or repress. If these are the only options, which one looks more "holy"? Repression. Yet there is another way! Rather than repressing lust by pushing it into the subconscious, trying to ignore it, or otherwise seeking to annihilate it, we must *surrender* our lusts to Christ and allow him to crucify them. As we do, the Spirit of the Lord gives new form to our desires. As we allow lust to be crucified, we also come to experience the resurrection of God's original plan for eros. Gradually, progressively, as we take up our cross every day and follow, we pass through various (and sometimes painful) purifications—and through it all, we come to experience sexual desire as the power to love in God's image.

This process of transformation requires not only a resolute will but also a firm faith. It's the Holy Spirit who transforms our hearts, who "reinflates our tires," who fills us with "new wine." And faith, you may recall, is the openness of the human heart to God's gift of the Holy Spirit.

When lust tempts you, or even overwhelms you, you might say a prayer like this:

> *Lord, I thank you for the gift of my sexual desires. I surrender this lustful desire to you, and I ask you please, by the power of your death and resurrection, to untwist in me what sin has twisted so that I might come to experience sexual desire as you created it to be—as the desire to love in your image.*

Death and Resurrection of Desire

To reinforce your decision to die to lust, you may also want to place yourself in the shape of a cross—hands outstretched—while offering the above prayer. The point here is to conform ourselves to Christ, to "carry around in our body the death of Jesus, so that the life of Jesus may also be revealed in our body" (2 Cor. 4:10).

Resolving *not* to indulge lust can be very difficult—at times even emotionally and physically wrenching. It seems few men and women experience the freedom for which Christ has set us free because when they taste this kind of crucifixion, rather than staying the course that leads to resurrection, they "come down from the cross." When those nails are biting into your hands and the burden of the cross seems too heavy to bear, keep going! You are on the verge of a passover from death to life, from lust to authentic love. Only if we are willing to die with Christ can we also live the resurrected life he offers.

C. S. Lewis shares a powerful image of this death and resurrection at the end of his book *The Great Divorce*. Before he can enter heaven, a human ghost must contend with the vice of lust, symbolized by a red lizard perched on the ghost's shoulder. When the Angel of Fire who guards the eternal gates asks permission to slay the lizard, we can all relate to the ghost's long list of excuses: not today; the gradual process is better; it will hurt too much; it might kill me; let me get an opinion from another doctor; and so on. Weighing the alternatives and realizing it would be better to be dead than to live with this vice, the ghost at long last grants permission. The Angel of Fire immediately grabs the lizard, twists its back, breaks its neck, and flings it to the ground.

As soon as the lizard is slain, the ghost takes on radiant flesh, a resurrected man, and pure love flows out of him "like liquid," says Lewis. But that's not even the best part. The lizard is also resurrected—now transformed into a great white stallion with a tail and mane of gold. The gates of heaven open, the resurrected man mounts the stallion, and redeemed eros itself is what enables him to climb the "impossible steeps" of life everlasting.

"What is a lizard compared with a stallion?" asks Lewis. "Lust is a weak, poor, whimpering, whispering thing compared with the richness and energy of desire which will arise when lust has been killed."[38] When lust has been *killed*. Perhaps we cling to lust in our lives because we're convinced that starvation is the only alternative to the fast food. But if God has prepared a banquet for us, an everlasting wedding feast that satisfies the deepest cry of eros beyond our wildest imaginings, then dying to lust means we *lose nothing* and *gain everything*, while clinging to lust means we *gain nothing* and *lose everything*. It's our choice.

Dear God, grant us the grace to choose you!

Discerning the Movements of Our Hearts

Let me emphasize—if this is not clear enough already—that the positive approach to purity I am outlining with John Paul II's help does not provide a license to push the envelope. The person who uses anything in this book as an excuse to indulge lust is not seeking purity. Honest people know their limits. They know what situations would make them stumble and avoid them with the seriousness Christ demands of us. "If your right eye causes you to stumble, gouge it out. . . . If your right hand causes you to stumble, cut it off" (Matt. 5:29–30). Modern adaptation: "If your smartphone causes you to sin, throw it away. If your laptop causes you to sin, get rid of it."

It's true that sometimes love and lust are difficult to distinguish. A man, for example, upon recognizing a woman's beauty, might wonder where the line is between seeing her as an object for his own gratification and properly admiring her beauty as a person made in God's image. As experience attests, lust "is not always plain and obvious; sometimes it is concealed, so that it passes itself off as 'love.' . . . Does this mean that we should distrust the human heart? No!" John Paul II insists. "It is only to say that we must remain in control of it."[39]

Control here doesn't mean merely dominating unruly desires in order to keep them in check. Again, that is only the negative side of the picture. As we mature in self-control, we experience it as "*the ability to orient* [sexual] reactions, both as to their content and as to their character."[40] The person who is truly master of himself is able to direct eros "toward what is true, good, and beautiful, so that what is 'erotic' also becomes true, good, and beautiful."[41] As this happens, we come to understand and experience the mystery of sexuality "in a depth, simplicity, and beauty hitherto altogether unknown."[42]

Getting to this point demands perseverance and consistency in learning the meaning of our bodies, the meaning of our sexuality. We must learn this not only in the abstract, says John Paul II, although this, too, is necessary. More so, we must learn the true meaning of our sexuality in the interior reactions of our own hearts. This is a "science," he says, that can't really be learned from books alone, because it's a question of deep knowledge of our interior life. Deep in the heart, we learn to distinguish between what, on the one hand, composes the great riches of sexuality and sexual attraction and what, on the other hand, bears only the sign of lust. And although these internal movements of the heart can sometimes be confused with one another, we have been called by Christ to acquire a mature and complete evaluation. "It should be added that this task *can* be carried out and that it is truly worthy of man."[43]

Let's close this chapter with a prayer for purity:

Lord, help me to discern the movements of my heart. Help me to distinguish between the great riches of sexuality as you created it to be and the distortions of lust. I grant you permission, Lord, to lead me on the journey of full purification from all of my lusts. Take them, Lord. Crucify them so that I might come to experience the resurrection of sexual desire as you intend. Grant me a pure heart so that I might see you. Amen.

FOUR

WILL THERE BE SEX IN HEAVEN?

The climax of the story of redemption is the marriage supper of the Lamb (Rev. 19:9–10). If history began with a wedding in Eden and closes with one in the New Jerusalem, the biblical story runs from wedding to wedding, from temporal symbol to eternal reality.

—Dennis Kinlaw

Allow me to take you on the last leg of one of my backpacking trips. I've been trudging through the woods with nearly fifty pounds on my back for several days. Exposure to the elements and restless nights in a tent have taken their toll. I've successfully sidestepped a few timber rattlesnakes. Slipping on boulders a few days earlier scraped up my shins. Every bend of my left leg aggravates a sharp pain in my knee joint, and each placement of a foot reminds me that my open blisters will take a week to heal. But I'm almost there, and the sure hope of arrival keeps me going—one arduous step at a time. The elation of having completed the journey will soon be mine. *I can do this. I'm almost there. Keep going . . .*

Life's journey, even if it's painful and difficult, can be lived and even embraced if we know that it leads toward a goal glorious enough to justify the effort of getting there. Being human is not easy. The journey toward our destiny is not easy. But Christ gives us assurance of a glorious goal. He also gives us assurance that the sufferings of the journey are *nothing* compared to the glory that awaits us (see Rom. 8:18).

All of creation, Paul tells us—and this means the entire universe and all that it contains—waits "in eager expectation" for this glory to be revealed because "the creation itself will be liberated from its bondage to decay" (Rom. 8:19, 21). We know, in fact, that "the whole creation has been groaning as in the pains of childbirth" and that "we ourselves . . . groan inwardly as we wait eagerly for . . ." (Rom. 8:22–23)—as we wait *for what?* What is it we're waiting for? What is it that we're journeying toward? What *is* this glory, and how great must it be if Paul can say that it makes all human suffering (from the beginning of time till the end of time) "as nothing" compared to it?

This glory, this "everything" that we (and all the universe) are waiting for, yearning for, groaning for, laboring in the pangs of childbirth for, Paul calls "the redemption of our bodies" (Rom. 8:23). And it is precisely hope in the redemption *of our bodies* that saves us (see Rom. 8:24), that gives us a reason to *stay the journey* even when it's arduous.

In this chapter we will seek to paint a picture, as best we can, of the glory that awaits us in the ultimate realization of redemption when our bodies will be raised in glory, reunited with our souls, and taken into the eternal wedding feast (assuming we say yes to God's invitation). As Paul puts it, our goal is to have the eyes of our hearts enlightened, so that we may know the hope to which we are called, "the riches of his glorious inheritance" and what is "his incomparably great power" at work in us (Eph. 1:18–19).

The Third Key Word of Christ

Christ entered history in "the fullness of time" (Gal. 4:4 ESV). In this sense, if Christ is who he says he is (God in the flesh), Christ's time on earth two thousand years ago is the very fulcrum of human history. From this fulcrum, Christ wants to reveal to us who we really are, and he does so by pivoting in two directions. Historical men and women live in a tension between the two poles of our *origin* and our *destiny*. And this is where Christ calls us—in the here and now—to find our true selves: right in this tension.

In his discussion with the Pharisees about marriage in Matthew 19, Christ pivots toward *the beginning*; in his discussion with the Sadducees about marriage in Matthew 22, Christ pivots toward *the end*. In the former, Christ points us to the state of man and woman's relationship *before* sin. In the latter, Christ points us to the state of man and woman's relationship *beyond* sin. Returning to our image of the deflated tires, our destiny cannot be understood only as a return to the fully inflated state of the beginning. Our destiny introduces us to an entirely *new* dimension of human life, love, and sexuality beyond all understanding and description. Tires, you might say, will give way to *flight*.

Christ reveals this entirely new dimension of human existence when he says, "At the resurrection people will neither marry nor be given in marriage" (Matt. 22:30). This statement is the final of the three key words John Paul II examines in order to discover

73

a "total vision of man." We will look first at the expression "in the resurrection," and then we will examine what it means that we will not be given in marriage.

Heaven: A Bodily Experience

N. T. Wright criticizes the disembodied notion of "heaven" to which large numbers of Christians subscribe, he contends. According to Wright, such believers are dangerously ignoring the insistent affirmation of the Apostles' Creed: "we believe in the resurrection of the body."[1]

In keeping with this disincarnate view of heaven, many Christians tend to see the body as a shell that they are anxious to shed or even as a prison from which they hope to be liberated at death. This is *not* the biblical view of things. Rather, it's a view from the philosophy of Plato that has crept into the minds of many Christians. The truth about man's destiny, John Paul II writes, "cannot be understood as a state of the soul alone, separated (according to Plato, liberated) from the body." Instead, Scripture teaches that the afterlife "must be understood as *the definitively and perfectly 'integrated' state of man* brought about by a [perfect] union of the soul with the body."[2]

Our bodies will certainly be different in their resurrected state (recall that the disciples did not recognize Jesus after his resurrection; see Luke 24:15–16), but we will still have them! For "our citizenship is in heaven. And we eagerly await a Savior from there, the Lord Jesus Christ, who . . . will transform our lowly bodies so that they will be like his glorious body" (Phil. 3:20–21).

Of course, we often speak of the souls in heaven. When we buried my mother-in-law, I saw her body go into the ground, and I am confident that her soul is now enjoying some form of union with God. But the souls currently in heaven ("currently," of course, is a time-bound word that does not even apply to heaven) remain in an in-human state until the resurrection of their bodies. My mother-in-law's body is now returning to dust, as will all our bodies. But if God can gather up dust and breathe his life into it at the beginning of time, he can certainly do it again at the end of time.

The perfect reunion of body and soul is our only hope as human beings, for that's what we *are* as human beings: the union of body and soul. The separation of the two at death is entirely unnatural. As Peter Kreeft writes, "A soul without a body is exactly the opposite of what Plato thought it is. It is not free but bound. . . . That is why the resurrection of the body is . . . not a dispensable extra. When death separates the two we have a freak, a monster, an obscenity. That is why we are terrified of ghosts and corpses, though both are harmless: they are the obscenely separated aspects of what belongs together as one."[3]

The Spiritualized Body

Paul addressed the believers in Corinth who questioned the resurrection of the body: "But someone will ask, 'How are the dead raised? With what kind of body will they come?'" And Paul responds, "The body . . . is raised imperishable; . . . it is raised in glory; . . . it is raised in power; . . . it is raised a spiritual body. . . . For the perishable must clothe itself with the imperishable, and the mortal with immortality" (1 Cor. 15:35, 42–44, 53).

While it often seems odd to us (because of our constant temptation to separate the physical and the spiritual), for Paul both the body and the soul are capable of being spiritual. The spiritualization of the body means that "*the powers of the spirit will permeate the energies of the body.*"[4] And because the spirit that will permeate our bodies is not only our own human, created spirit but also the divine, uncreated Holy Spirit, John Paul II speaks also of the "divinization" (making divine) of the body. Following after the pattern of Christ's bodily ascension into the life of the Trinity, in the final reality we will participate, body and soul, in the eternal life of God. Our human nature, body and soul, will participate "in the divine nature" (2 Pet. 1:4).

Recall our earlier discussion of God's innermost secret: God himself is an eternal *communion of persons*—Father, Son, and Holy Spirit—and he has destined us to share in that eternal bliss. This is what we mean by the spiritualization and divinization of the body. To the degree that creatures can, we will share—body and soul—in God's eternal exchange of love. And this "profound mystery" is prefigured right from the beginning in man and woman's exchange of love—that is, in and through their union in one flesh.

So, many ask, will there be sex in heaven? It depends what we mean by the term. Sex is not first what people *do*. It is who people *are* as male or female, and nothing of our authentic humanity gets deleted in the resurrection. So, in this sense, yes, there will be sex in heaven inasmuch as we will be fully masculine and fully feminine. But, as we will learn from Christ's words about the resurrection, the union of the sexes as we know it now will give way to an *infinitely greater* union. Those who are raised in glory will experience a bliss so far superior to earthly sexual union that our wee brains cannot even begin to fathom it. Eye has not seen, ear has not heard, nor has it even dawned on us what God has prepared for those who love him (see 1 Cor. 2:9).

Pastor Rick Warren offers this reflection: "It always amazes me that God chose to bring people into the world through sex so that Jesus could bring them into heaven. Think about this: Jesus told us there's going to be no sex in heaven [as in, no sexual intercourse]. But without sex on earth there'd be no people to go to heaven."[5]

Christ Points Us to the Ultimate "Marriage"

At first glance, Christ's insistence that we will no longer marry in our resurrected state may seem to undermine all that we have said about the greatness of marital love and the sexual embrace. But examined more closely, these words point to the crowning glory of all we've said. Marriage exists from the beginning to point us to the marriage of the Lamb (see Rev. 19:7), to the union of Christ and the church (see Eph. 5:31–32).

As Bible scholar Dennis Kinlaw puts it, when the Bible speaks of "the New Jerusalem coming down out of heaven 'prepared as a bride beautifully dressed for her husband' (Rev. 21:2) . . . the human story that began with a wedding comes to its end; the wedding in the garden of Eden and every other wedding in human history . . . prefigured this end—a royal wedding—the one in which the Father gives a bride to his Son." This means that marriage was designed by God "to teach human creatures what human history is really all about."[6]

What's human history really all about? Marriage . . . to God. This is *why we exist*: to participate in the eternal exchange of love found in God by being wed eternally to his Son. This is why we have that *ache* inside of us that never quits in this life. That *something* we're looking for is the eternal bliss of being one with God. The union of the sexes—as beautiful and wonderful as it is in the divine plan—is only a faint glimmer, a pale picture within time, of that eternal union with God. In the resurrection, the original sign will give way to the divine reality. In other words, if God created the union of the sexes as a foreshadowing of heaven, then when Christ says we're no longer given in marriage in the resurrection, he's saying, "You no longer need a foreshadowing to point you *to* heaven when you are *in* heaven. You're there. The ultimate union has come."

People often ask, "Does this mean I won't be with my spouse in heaven?" Assuming both spouses say yes to God's wedding invitation, they will certainly be together. All who respond will live together in a communion that fulfills superabundantly all that is good, true, and beautiful about marriage and family life here on earth. What we need to understand is that the union of the sexes is not our be-all and end-all. It's only an icon, a sign of something infinitely greater. In other words, marriage does not express definitively the deepest meaning of sexuality. It merely provides a concrete expression of that meaning within history. At the end of history, the "historical" expression of sexuality will make way for an entirely new expression of our call to life-giving communion.

Icons and Idols

When we lose sight of that infinitely greater union, we inevitably treat the icon as an idol. In other words, when we lose sight of the joys of heaven, we tend to view sexual union and its pleasures as our ultimate fulfillment. Welcome to the world in which we live.

Still, there is an important element of truth in our society's idolatrous obsession with sex. Behind every false god we discover our desire for the true God gone awry. The sexual confusion so prevalent in our world and in our own hearts is actually the human desire for heaven gone berserk. Untwist the distortions and we discover the astounding glory of sex in the divine plan. "For this reason . . . the two will become one flesh" (Matt. 19:5; cf. Gen 2:24). For what reason? To reveal, proclaim, and anticipate the eternal union of Christ and the church (see Eph. 5:31–32).

"Sin" means to "miss the mark." It's an archer's term. So is the word "destiny": it means "to aim at." When we sin, we're actually aiming for something good, but we miss the target. And when that target is heaven, that's a mark we really don't want to miss!

We might put it this way: God gave us eros as the fuel of a rocket that's meant to launch us to the stars (to infinity and beyond!). Yet what would happen if the engines of that rocket became inverted, pointing us back upon ourselves and no longer toward the stars? Launch that rocket and the result is a massive blast of self-destruction. Herein we discover the importance of Christ's words about the new state of the body and sex in the resurrection: they help us set our sights on the union that alone can satisfy. As we allow the power of these words to sink into our hearts, they begin to redirect our rocket engines toward the stars. In turn, the idol once again can become the icon it was meant to be.

This is the *redemption* of desire. We shouldn't be discouraged by how often we miss the mark. Here we should never forget that desire itself can be transformed and redirected. The purification that we all need in this regard is not about suffocating eros but about allowing it to reach its true height; it's not about turning desire down but about turning it up, way up: toward the stars! As C. S. Lewis put it:

Indeed, if we consider the unblushing promises of reward and the staggering nature of the rewards promised in the Gospels, it would seem that our Lord finds our desires, not too strong, but too weak. We are half-hearted creatures, fooling about with drink and sex and ambition when infinite joy is offered us, like an ignorant child who wants to go on making mud pies in a slum because he cannot imagine what is meant by the offer of a holiday at the sea. We are far too easily pleased.[7]

Only to the degree that eros is aimed toward "the stars" does marriage take on its true meaning as a sign and foreshadowing of Christ's love for the church. Marriage, when properly lived, gives us a taste of heaven on earth. But when heaven comes, signs and foreshadowings give way to the reality. There will be no marriage in heaven not because it will be *deleted* but because it will be eternally *completed* in the marriage of the Lamb. This should not cause sadness but rejoicing. Every human longing, every desire of the heart for love and union will be fulfilled beyond our wildest dreams. That deep ache of solitude will finally be completely and eternally satisfied.

Experience attests that even the most wonderful marriage does not fully satisfy our hunger for love and union. We still yearn for something more. I love my wife, Wendy, more than any words can express, but she will not mind my saying that she is not my ultimate fulfillment. We must not hang our hats on a hook that cannot bear the weight! If we look to another human person as our ultimate fulfillment, we will crush that person. Only the eternal, ecstatic marriage of heaven—so far superior to anything proper to earthly life that we cannot begin to fathom it—can satisfy the human ache of solitude.

Anticipating the Kingdom

Helping us to direct our desire for lasting peace and happiness solely toward the kingdom is an integral part of the inner logic of Paul's often-quoted and often-misunderstood teaching in 1 Corinthians 7 about marriage and singleness. In so many words, Paul suggests that those who are married should live as though they weren't and that those who are not should remain single as he is. Tim Keller summarizes Paul's inner logic well: "We are to be neither overly elated about getting married nor overly disappointed about not being so—because Christ is the only spouse who can truly fulfill us and God's family the only family that will truly embrace and satisfy us." The Bible's "exalted view of marriage . . . points to the true marriage that our souls need and the true family our hearts want. No [earthly] marriage can give us what we most desire and truly need."[8]

The more we realize that the deep longing we feel as human beings can only be satisfied in the eternal kingdom, the more we realize, whether we're married or single, that the pressure is off. Married people: the pressure is off for you to be your spouse's perfect fulfillment. You can't possibly be (guess who already knows that: your spouse!). Single people: the pressure is off for you to find that "special someone" in order to be happy. The happiness we're looking for can be found only in the marriage of Christ and the church, and that is something already offered to us. In fact, Christ explicitly calls some men and women to remain unmarried in order to give themselves wholly and entirely, even now, to the heavenly marriage.

"For there are eunuchs who were born that way, and there are eunuchs who have been made eunuchs by others—and there are those who choose to live like eunuchs for the sake of the kingdom of heaven" (Matt. 19:12). A eunuch is someone physically incapable of sexual relations. But a eunuch for the kingdom of heaven is someone who freely forgoes sexual relations in anticipation of the ultimate reality to which sexual relations point: the eternal union of Christ and the church. In this way, those who take up Christ's call to remain unmarried explicitly for the kingdom do not reject their sexuality. They're showing the rest of the world the ultimate purpose and meaning of sexuality: to point us to union with God.

The spousal meaning of the body reveals that the human person is created to be a gift "for" another. Christ's words quoted above show that this "for," which stands at the basis of marriage, can also stand at the basis of remaining unmarried "for" the kingdom of heaven. All people are called to prepare themselves for eternal union with God. Christian celibacy, as "the self-giving of a human person wedded to God himself, expressly anticipates this eternal union with God and points the way to it."[9]

Of course, the normal way to prepare for the heavenly marriage is through earthly marriage. But some are given a special grace to "skip" earthly marriage and go straight for the heavenly reality. And as Jesus says, "The one who can accept this should accept it" (Matt. 19:12). It's in this light that Paul tells the Corinthians, "It is good . . . to stay unmarried, as I do" (1 Cor. 7:8).

Matthew Lee Anderson correctly observes that the "idea of a vocation—or a calling—to lifelong celibacy for the kingdom of God does not minimize the importance of marriage. Each calling bears witness to different aspects of our world. Oliver O'Donovan puts it this way: '[The New Testament church] conceived of marriage and singleness as alternative vocations, each a worthy form of life, the two together comprising the whole Christian witness. . . . The one declared that God had vindicated the order of creation, the other pointed beyond it to its eschatological transformation.' In other words, marriage points to Genesis, singleness to Revelation."[10]

The clear but often neglected biblical truths about celibacy for the kingdom can also be a source of great consolation for those who may not have chosen to remain single but find themselves unable to marry for some reason. Accepting this difficult situation in a spirit of trust can be the occasion of awakening a *living hope* in the resurrection when "the absolute and eternal spousal meaning of the glorified body will be revealed in union with God himself."[11] "Then you will look and be radiant, your heart will throb and swell with joy" (Isa. 60:5). Never again will you hunger; never again will you thirst. For the Bridegroom will lead you to springs of living water and wipe away every tear from your eyes (see Rev. 7:16–17). Now we hope in all these things, but we see only dimly, "we see only a reflection as in a mirror; then we shall see face to face. Now I know in part; then I shall know fully, even as I am fully known" (1 Cor. 13:12).

The Vision of God: Participation in Divine Beauty

As C. S. Lewis insightfully expressed, "We do not want merely to see beauty, though, God knows, even that is bounty enough. We want something else which can hardly be put into words—to be united with the beauty we see, to pass into it, to receive it into ourselves, to bathe in it, to become part of it."[12] This gives us a sense of what "seeing God face-to-face" will entail: we will *know* his beauty in the deepest biblical sense of that word, and it will fill all who behold the divine glory with never-ending ecstasy.

Recall man and woman's original face-to-face vision of each other. This provides a faint glimmer or prefigurement of the vision of love that awaits us in heaven. Before sin, man and woman were naked without shame because their vision was infused with an uncompromised love. Man and woman had no fear of being fully "seen" because each loved and received the other in the full truth of his or her naked humanity. Their mutual vision expressed

83

their profound, personal "knowledge" of each other. They participated in the sheer goodness of each other's humanity.

John Paul II writes that the eternal vision of heaven is "a concentration of knowledge . . . and love on God himself." This knowledge "cannot be anything but full participation in God's inner life, that is, in trinitarian Reality itself."[13] In the resurrection, we will *know* God, and he will *know* us (he already does, of course). We will participate fully—insofar as creatures can—in God's divinity, and he will participate fully in our humanity (he already does, of course, having taken on human nature in the incarnation).

God has humbled himself to share in our humanity so that we might share in his own divine life. What a glorious exchange! We give God our humanity, and he gives us his divinity. This, of course, does not mean that we will lose our human nature and become on par with God. It does mean, though, that God will give us a share in his own divinity, to the degree that our humanity will allow.

This divine-human exchange expresses something of the content or inner dynamic of the eternal vision of heaven. Recall here that this is exactly what the serpent convinced us God was withholding—his divine life and our happiness. "If you want to be 'like God,'" he insinuated, "you need to *take* it, because God sure ain't gonna give it to you." No! God has always desired for us to share fully in his own divinity. It's a free gift! All we need to do is open our humanity and *receive* it. We need not grasp at what God freely gives us. Sin—and all human misery—begins right here, with grasping at the gift.

Fulfillment of the Spousal Meaning of the Body

How will this glorious exchange between God and man take place? Since the nuptials of heaven are beyond all human knowledge, all we can do is speculate. Yet, once again, we see a faint glimmer of what is to come in the nuptials of earth.

The original exchange of man and woman took place through the "freedom of the gift" and the "spousal meaning of the body." Recall that God's gift of freedom to us is the capacity to love. Without freedom, it's impossible to make a gift of ourselves to others—that is, it's impossible to love. Furthermore, God inscribed this call to self-donation right in our bodies as male and female. Our bodies have a "spousal meaning" because they are capable of expressing divine love, *precisely that love in which the person becomes a gift* and—through this gift—fulfills the very meaning of his being and existence."[14]

In the resurrection we discover—in a new, heavenly dimension—the same spousal meaning of the body. This time, however, the spousal meaning of the body is fulfilled in our meeting with the mystery of the living God, through our vision of him face-to-face. Applying the spousal analogy, we can conclude that in the resurrection, the divine Bridegroom will express his gift ("this is my body given for you") in its fullest reality. All who respond to the wedding invitation will open their humanity to receive this gift as Christ's bride. In response to this gift, we will give ourselves totally to the divine Bridegroom in an eternally life-giving embrace.

This is the cry of the bride, in union with the Spirit, when together, in the very final verses of the Bible, they say, "Come! . . . Come, Lord Jesus!" (see Rev. 22:17, 20). The bride longs, aches, pines to be united with her Bridegroom in the rapture of love that never ends. Indeed, she is "faint with love": she is at the point of passing out in her longing for it (see Song 2:5).

In the marriage of the Lamb, "penetration and permeation of what is essentially human by what is essentially divine will then reach its peak."[15] The sexual imagery is unmistakable. It may be rather scandalous to some, but as we've been seeing throughout this book, this kind of imagery is deeply biblical. Of course, when using erotic love as an image of heaven, it's especially important to remember the inadequacy of analogies. Heaven is not some eternally magnified experience of sexual union on earth. As John Paul II observes, the union to come "will be a completely new experience." Yet at the same time, he says, "it will not be alienated in any way" from the love that man and woman experienced in "the beginning" and have sought to reclaim throughout history.[16]

In the resurrection we will experience the ultimate fulfillment of the "redemption of our bodies" (Rom. 8:23). The original meaning of the body will then be revealed again in an *eternal splendor*, when all who respond to the wedding invitation will live in the full freedom of self-giving love. Those whose bodies rise to eternal life will experience "the absolute and eternal spousal meaning of the glorified body . . . in union with God himself."[17]

The Communion of Saints

We will live out this self-giving love not only as individuals in union with God. As alluded to earlier, we will also live in self-giving love and communion with all the saints, who enjoy the eternal vision of God. Recall that, in his experience of solitude, Adam discovered his fundamental vocation: love of God *and* love of neighbor. Heaven fulfills both dimensions of this vocation. When we reach our ultimate destiny we will live in consummate union with all who are raised in glory.

This consummation will be the ultimate realization of the unity of the human race, which God willed from "the beginning" when he called man and woman to become "one body." In this way, sexual union in God's plan "points to the eternal ecstasy of soul that we will have in heaven in our loving relationships with God and one another," as Tim Keller puts it.[18] Heaven will be the experience of a great multitude of glorified men and women "from every nation, tribe, people and language" (Rev. 7:9) united eternally in one body (see 1 Cor. 12:20). This union obviously will not be experienced in the sexual sense lived by a husband and wife here on earth. Yet we can conclude that in some mysterious way beyond earthly comprehension, all that is masculine in our humanity will be in union with all that is feminine in our humanity. That unity—that "one body"—will be the one bride of Christ living in consummate union with her Bridegroom forever.

In and through this communion with Christ, the communion of the redeemed will live in communion with *the* Communion, the Trinity. We will *see* all and *be seen* by all. We will *know* all and *be known* by all—and God will be "all in all" (Eph. 1:23 RSV). John Eldredge expressed the same idea when he wrote that the "naked intimacy, the real knowing that we enjoy with God, we shall enjoy with each other." He suggests that we might call it "multiple intimacy without promiscuity. It is what the ancients meant by the communion of saints." He continues:

The setting for this will be a great party, the wedding feast of the Lamb. . . . There is *dancing*: "The maidens will dance and be glad, young men, and old as well" (Jer. 31:13). There is *feasting*: "On this mountain the Lord Almighty will prepare a feast of rich food for all peoples" (Isa. 25:6). And there is *drinking*— the feast God says he is preparing includes "a banquet of aged wines—the best of meats and the finest of wines" (Isa. 25:6). In fact, at his Last Supper our Bridegroom said he will not drink of "the fruit of the vine until the kingdom of God comes" (Luke 22:18). Then he'll pop the cork.[19]

Once when I was trying to explain these concepts in class, one of my students replied, "It sounds like you're describing a drunken orgy or something." "*No!*" I insisted. A drunken orgy is a diabolic mockery of the communion of saints. Remember that the devil doesn't have his own clay. All he can do is take God's clay and twist it, distort it, mock it. And his mockeries have done such a number on us that when the holy and sacred realities are presented, we almost instantly associate them with his diabolical distortions.

Satan is the great plagiarizer. He takes the holy things of God and puts his name on them. Tragically, many Christians, fleeing the flesh in favor of a disembodied spirituality, are content to let the enemy have what he's stolen. The TOB is a clarion call for Christians to reclaim what Satan has plagiarized. Sex belongs to God. It was his idea. He invented it. And, as if it needs to be said again, he did so for *this* purpose: to prefigure in some way the glory, ecstasy, and bliss that awaits us in heaven (see Eph. 5:31–32). No wonder we are all so interested in sex! God put an innate desire in every human being to want to understand the meaning of sexuality, and he did so to lead us to him. That's exactly why the enemy attacks right here, to derail our search for the banquet.

Our God Is Rich in Mercy

For lack of knowledge of this divine wedding feast, we tend to oscillate between starving eros and binging on the fast food. In either case, while we might manage to put on a happy face to get by, underneath we find no shortage of misery. The good news of the gospel is that our God is rich in mercy, which means *he is drawn to us in our misery*. The Latin for mercy, *misericordia*, actually means "a heart that gives itself to those in misery."

If you've taken a repressive approach to desire, you might want to pray something like this:

Lord, I have been afraid of my desire. I have been afraid that living from that "fire" inside me would only cause me pain or lead me astray. Awaken a holy and noble eros in me, Lord. Give me the courage to feel it and help me to experience it as my desire for your fire. Help me also to rejoice rightly in the many gifts and pleasures of this life as so many "signs" of the joy that awaits me in heaven. Amen.

If you've taken an indulgent approach to desire, you might want to pray:

Lord, I have taken my desire to things that cannot satisfy. I have not known how to remain in my "ache" for you, how to wait on you, how to trust in you—so I have grasped at a great many pleasures apart from you. Please help me redirect my desire from the finite pleasures of this world to the infinite ecstasy that awaits me in heaven, and help me to recognize all the good things you have made in this world as so many "icons" pointing me to you. Amen.

Why was Christ so compassionate toward sexual sinners, especially women? I think it was because, behind their deception, he knew they were looking for him, the true Bridegroom.

Think of the woman caught in adultery (see John 8:2–11). She went looking for love, intimacy, and union with another; but, as always, the counterfeit couldn't satisfy. Laden with shame, she was brought before Christ by an angry crowd anxious to stone her. Christ then said that whoever was without sin could cast the first stone. According to his own words, the sinless Christ could have thrown a stone. But Christ came not to condemn; he came to save (see John 3:17).

The Gospel adds the detail that Jesus stayed with the woman until everyone in the angry mob had gone and "only Jesus was left, with the woman still standing there" (John 8:9). What happened next, when the woman was alone with the divine Bridegroom? Reading into the story a bit, we can imagine that she had a conversion from the counterfeit to the real thing. Do you think when Jesus said, "Go now and leave your life of sin" (John 8:11), that she turned and grumbled, "Who is this man to tell me what I can and cannot do with my body"? Or do you think, having encountered the love she was truly looking for, she left transformed, renewed, and affirmed in the deepest part of her being as a woman?

What are the lies you have believed about your body, about the bodies of others, about the meaning of sex? What are the counterfeits you have bought into? Behind them all is your authentic thirst for love. Sexual sin is a quest to satisfy that thirst with "dead water." Christ meets us right there without condemnation: "If you knew the gift of God . . . you would have asked him and he would have given you living water" (John 4:10).

Like so many of us, the woman at the well didn't know the gift of God, so she had taken her thirst elsewhere: "You have had five husbands, and the man you now have is not your husband" (John 4:18). Six lovers. Do you see the symbolism? Six is the imperfect biblical number. Seven is the perfect biblical number. Who is this woman's seventh lover? Christ, the Bridegroom! His love is what she's been thirsting for the whole time—a "living water" welling up to eternal life (see John 4:1–36).

How tender Jesus is with our broken humanity! We must not fear to throw our wounded sexuality wide open to Christ, to invite his healing, merciful love to come in to all of our diseased images and painful memories so that he can "touch our wounds." Christ *never* robs us of our humanity. He restores it to us. He comes not to impose rules on us but to teach us tenderly the ways of authentic love. Being Christian is not about conforming our lives to a list of rules or a code of ethics. It's about the encounter with a Person who can radically change our lives, heal our wounds, and transform our desires, redirecting eros toward "the stars."

Following Christ is "a journey totally sustained by grace," as John Paul II affirms. It also "demands an intense spiritual commitment and is no stranger to painful purifications."[20] But like the challenge of a backpacking trip, if we keep putting one foot in front of the other, we'll make it to our destiny. Life, even if it's difficult, can be lived and even embraced if we know it leads toward a goal glorious enough to justify the effort of getting there.

What's the goal that justifies all the trials, struggles, and sufferings of this life? Where does this crazy journey lead? To being "wholly possessed by the divine Beloved," John Paul II tells us, "to the ineffable joy experienced by the mystics as 'nuptial union'" *with God*.[21] This is the eternal ecstasy, unrivaled rapture, and bounteous, beauteous bliss for which we yearn with all our being.

Lord, grant us faith. Help us believe in this glorious gift. And help us stay the journey, come what may. Amen.

FIVE

THIS IS A PROFOUND MYSTERY

A man leaves his parents, who gave him life, and is joined to his
wife, and one flesh—father, mother, and child—results from
the commingling of the two. . . . Our relationship to Christ is
similar; we become one flesh with him through communion . . .
[and] this has been his plan from the beginning.

—John Chrysostom

I remember how excited I was in the fall of 2004 to return from
a business trip in New York City to tell Wendy what had just
happened. The biggest publishing house in the world had just
offered me a really attractive book deal. They wanted me to
write a book for husbands called *Loving Her Rightly*.

Expecting her to rejoice with me at this great opportunity, I
was rather stunned when her face immediately fell upon hear-
ing the title of the book. "What's wrong?" I asked. Wendy responded, "You and I need to talk . . . and it's gonna be long,

and it's gonna be painful." "What do you mean?" I asked, be-wildered. "Let me just put it to you this way," she said: "You are in *no place* to be writing a book for husbands called *Loving Her Rightly*!"

Oh! If I had given voice to the pride that wanted to raise its ugly head in me (*Wait a minute—you're married to the "Theology of the Body guy"!*), it would have been quite a scene. Instead, by the grace of God, I swallowed my pride and listened to her. In fact, for several months, I arranged to have someone watch the kids once a week so we could have time to talk. Actually, for the most part, Wendy talked, and I just listened. It was time for me to hear from my wife what ten years of being married to the "Theology of the Body guy" had been like for her.

She was right: it was *long*, and it was *painful*. Amid plenty of "wheat" in our relationship, there were also lots of "weeds," and instead of tending to them, I was traveling the world telling other people about the TOB.

When I got married in the mid-nineties, I had already been studying and sharing the TOB with others for about two years. Married life has taught me that it's one thing to have lots of good theology *about* God's plan for marriage in your head. It's another thing to *live it*. It's one thing to write books, give lectures, and teach classes on the Theology of the Body; it's another thing to walk through the painful purifications that are an absolutely necessary part of the journey. Praise God for his mercy, and for my wife's!

The First Ingredient for a Successful Marriage

The number one ingredient for a successful marriage is mercy. We must keep this in mind as we venture into this section of our Bible study. For, if we choose to marry, we "must choose it exactly as it was instituted by the Creator 'from the beginning.'"[1] And all of us must contend with a host of faults, failings, and weaknesses that cause us to fall short of that glory. Is it even possible for couples to reclaim the original splendor of God's plan? "With man this is impossible, but with God all things are possible" (Matt. 19:26).

As we continue, we will see more clearly that marriage plunges spouses right into the heart of the mystery of our redemption in Christ: the mystery through which we discover that God's grace is sufficient for us, for his power is made perfect in our weakness (see 2 Cor. 12:9). And this means that there "is no need to be dismayed if love sometimes follows torturous ways. Grace has power to make straight the paths of human love."[2]

Mystery and Sacrament

Before we continue, it's important to establish a distinction between marriage as a Sacrament in the strict sense of the term and marriage as a sacrament in the broader, more ancient sense of the term. Luther believed there were only two Sacraments in the strict sense of the term: baptism and communion. Catholics, Orthodox, and many Anglicans believe there are seven Sacraments, marriage being one of them. Exploring the theological differences among Christians regarding marriage as a Sacrament is beyond the scope of this book. We can all find agreement, however, in applying the broader, more ancient definition of sacrament to marriage when we understand its relation to Paul's teaching in Ephesians 5:31–32.

"'For this reason a man will leave his father and mother and be united to his wife, and the two will become one flesh.' This is a profound mystery—but I am talking about Christ and the church" (Eph. 5:31–32). When Paul's letters were translated from Greek to Latin, the term *mysterion* was often rendered *sacramentum*. Holding the different nuances of these two words together—"mystery-sacrament"—gives us a more complete picture of the astounding truths Paul is seeking to communicate in his letter to the Ephesians.

Recall that Paul wants to "make plain to everyone" the "mystery, which for ages past was kept hidden in God" (Eph. 3:9). Making God's mystery "plain" is what a sacrament does. And it does so through a physical sign. For Paul, that sign, that sacrament, is the body in its masculinity and femininity, in its call to union. Paul, in fact, is able to explain the "whole reality [of redemption], which is essentially spiritual and supernatural, through the likeness of the body and of the love by which . . . husband and wife become 'one flesh.'"[3] It's in this way that he makes God's mystery "plain to everyone" in Ephesians 5.

And yet, even when God's mystery is revealed, made known, made plain through this sign, it's still a *mystery*. For we can never exhaust the infinitude of God: the more his mystery is known, the more we know that there is more to know. In short, we can say that, together, these words—"mystery-sacrament"— refer to the "hidden-revealed" dimensions of God and his plan for humanity. The good news of the gospel is that the mystery *hidden* in God from eternity has been *revealed*—the *mystery* has become a *sacrament*, a visible sign of an invisible reality.

In the beginning, God's mystery became visible through the great sign of man and woman's union in marriage. In the "fullness of time" this same mystery became visible through the new sign of Christ's union with the church. As we will come to understand more deeply in this chapter, the divinely inspired genius of Paul in Ephesians 5 is that "he brought these two signs together, making of them *the single great sign*."[4] These two "great signs"—the union of husband-wife and the union of Christ-church—express *one mystery* and, thus, form one "great sacrament." All of this is contained in Paul's marvelous teaching.

In this chapter we will look more closely at the mystery—the divine gift that is communicated through marriage. In the next chapter we will look more closely at the sacrament—the human sign of married love through which the divine gift is communicated.

The Crowning Theme of All the Themes in Scripture

It is virtually impossible to overstate how important Ephesians 5 is in the history of Christian theology. In our prayerful examination of this text, we must try "to understand if possible 'to the very depths' what wealth of the truth revealed by God is contained within the scope of [this] stupendous page."[5] By showing us the heart of God's spousal love for us, this "key and classic text," as John Paul II describes it, not only immerses us in the glory and greatness of God's plan for creating us male and female and calling us to become one flesh, it also serves as "the compendium or *summa*, in some sense, *of the teaching about God and man* which was brought to fulfillment by Christ."[6]

And so we find in the "profound mystery" of Ephesians 5 the crowning theme of all the themes in Sacred Scripture—the "central reality" of the whole of divine revelation. Here we find what God "wishes above all to transmit to mankind in his Word."[7] As we've been saying throughout this book, God wants to marry us.

While the prophets spoke very boldly of God's spousal love for Israel, this mystery was only "half-open" in the Old Testament. In Ephesians 5, the mystery of God's spousal love is "fully unveiled (without ceasing to be a mystery, of course)."⁸ In turn, we become witnesses "of a particular encounter of [God's] mystery with the very essence of the vocation to marriage."⁹

Here is the entire passage:

> Submit to one another out of reverence for Christ.
>
> Wives, submit to your husbands as to the Lord. For the husband is the head of the wife as Christ is the head of the church, his body, of which he is the Savior. Now as the church submits to Christ, so also wives should submit to their husbands in everything.
>
> Husbands, love your wives, just as Christ loved the church and gave himself up for her to make her holy, cleansing her by the washing with water through the word, and to present her to himself as a radiant church, without stain or wrinkle or any other blemish, but holy and blameless. In this same way, husbands ought to love their wives as their own bodies. He who loves his wife loves himself. After all, no one ever hated their own body, but they feed and care for their body, just as Christ does the church—for we are members of his body. "For this reason a man will leave his father and mother and be united to his wife, and the two will become one flesh." This is a profound mystery—but I am talking about Christ and the church. However, each one of you also must love his wife as he loves himself, and the wife must respect her husband. (Eph. 5:21–33)

That Controversial Line

If we are to mine the riches of Paul's teaching on the "profound mystery" of marriage, we would do well to address head-on the fact that Ephesians 5 contains one of the most controversial lines in the whole Bible: "Wives, submit to your husbands." In Christian circles today, approaches to this passage usually lean in one of two directions. Many dismiss Paul's teaching out of hand as nothing but a product of the chauvinism of his time, as if it had nothing whatsoever to say to us in a modern context. Others appeal to Paul's teaching on "submission" to justify a terribly distorted approach to leadership in marriage that amounts to little more than a veiled form of male domination. By reading the passage in context—both the overall context of Scripture and the cultural context in which Paul was writing—we find a very balanced and compelling reading of Paul's teaching on submission that avoids errors on both sides.

First we must recognize that Scripture clearly reveals the tendency of men to dominate women as a specific result of original sin. Before sin, the original order of love called the husband to "initiate" the gift of self in the image of God. The woman, in turn, recognizing the sincerity of her husband's gift, longed to receive it and to return it, thus forming a true "communion of persons." Only *after* original sin, and only as a result of it, does God say to the woman, "Your desire will be for your husband, and he will rule over you" (Gen. 3:16). The verbs translated as "desire" and "rule" both indicate the tragic effects of sin on man and woman's original communion. The man's initiation of the gift has warped into men's sinful tendency to dominate women; and the woman's longing to receive and to return the sincere gift of herself has warped into a tendency toward manipulative self-interest.

As we will see, Paul is in no way justifying these sinful tendencies in marriage. Quite the contrary: he's calling spouses *back to the original order of love* through the redemption won for them in Christ.

Paul's Evangelical Genius

Like all of us, Paul was certainly affected by his culture. As John Paul II writes, he "is not afraid to accept the concepts that were characteristic of the mentality and customs of that time. . . . Certainly, our contemporary sensitivity is different, . . . and the social position of women in comparison with men is different."[10] But if we simply dismiss Paul's words as nothing but a product of his politically incorrect culture, we miss his evangelical genius altogether. Like any great teacher, Paul appeals to the language and customs of the culture he is trying to reach while injecting that language and those customs with the mystery of Christ.

In the preceding chapter of his letter (remember, *context* is key), Paul states explicitly, and "insist[s] on it in the Lord," that Christians "must no longer live as the Gentiles do, in the futility of their thinking. They are darkened in their understanding . . . due to the hardening of their hearts." They "indulge in every kind of impurity." So the Ephesians are told "to put off your old self, which is being corrupted by its deceitful [other translations say "lustful"] desires; to be made new in the attitude of your minds; and to put on the new self, created to be like God in true righteousness and holiness" (Eph. 4:17–19, 22–24).

This should all sound very familiar to us by now. Who also spoke of "hardness of heart" and how it distorts the sexual relationship? Who also invited men and women to live in "true righteousness and holiness" by experiencing redemption from lustful desires? Like Christ, Paul is calling men and women to live according to the divine image in which God originally made them—and he's pointing them to Christ as the Savior who enables them to do so.

When the contested verses of Ephesians 5 are read in their full context, we realize that—far from demeaning women and absolving abusive men—Paul is restoring the only sure foundation for the proper balance of love between the sexes. In effect, Paul is saying something like this: "Sure, since this is the language you are used to, we can talk about 'submission' in marriage. But that means one thing to the Gentiles. Here is how it must look for followers of Christ."

Mutual Submission out of Reverence for Christ

Notice the first thing Paul says about submission in Ephesians 5: "Submit to *one another* out of reverence for Christ" (v. 21). Although this line seems to have been largely forgotten, it is clear that the Bible calls spouses to a *mutual* submission. Those who think Paul was simply regurgitating cultural prejudice against women do not understand how countercultural this idea was.

John Paul II insists that the apostle "does not intend to say that . . . marriage is a contract of domination by the husband over the wife. . . . Love makes the *husband simultaneously subject* to the wife."[11] He adds that being subject to one's spouse means being "completely given." Therefore, mutual submission means a reciprocal gift of self.[12] It means both spouses realize and live the spousal meaning of their bodies, which calls them to mutual and sincere self-giving.

It's clear that Christ must be the source and the model of this self-giving, since Paul calls spouses to give themselves up for one another "out of reverence for Christ" (v. 21). We can even say that this reverence is none other than a "*spiritually mature form*" of the mutual attraction of the sexes, of that "*fascination* of the man for femininity and of the woman for masculinity."[13] In other words, "reverence for Christ" results from a lived experience of the redemption of sexual attraction and desire, the redemption of eros. Through ongoing growth and healing, we gradually come to experience that mature level of purity we spoke of previously.

Pure men and women *see* the mystery of Christ revealed through their bodies. It's not just a theory or concept; pure men

101

and women *feel* it in their hearts. They realize that the call to union inscribed in their sexuality is a "profound mystery" that proclaims the union of Christ and the church. To the degree that we experience this as the content of our sexual attractions, we do not want to lust—we want to *bow*. To the degree that we live as Paul calls us to, lust becomes distasteful to us. The "profound mystery" of sexuality fills us instead with deep amazement, awe, and wonder. In other words, it fills us with *reverence for Christ*.

In turn, this reverence for the "profound mystery" revealed through our sexuality opens up realms of freedom and joy previously inaccessible to us. We come to possess ourselves and our passions. Eros is no longer in control of us; we are in control of it. And, in delightful freedom, we're able to direct erotic desire toward the sincere gift of self. "The satisfaction of the passions is, in fact, one thing, quite another is the joy a person finds in possessing himself more fully, since in this way he can also become more fully a true gift for another person."[14]

Of course, there is always an ever-deeper need for purification in this regard. One can never consider self-mastery acquired once and for all. The "reverence for Christ" that the Bible calls us to in our sexuality presupposes renewed effort at all stages of life. But the effort it requires repays us a thousandfold in finding the "freedom [for which] Christ has set us free" (Gal. 5:1) and in coming to taste the love and joy for which our hearts truly long.

Submission within the Spousal Analogy

If Paul is only regurgitating the cultural idea of wives as the property of their husbands, the feminist revolt against Ephesians 5 is quite understandable. In the absence of redemption, Paul's words can only be viewed as an admonition for wives to resign themselves to male lust and tyranny. But redemption has been accomplished! The knowledge that Christ died and rose again to empower us to live according to God's original plan of love deeply imbues the apostle's entire teaching on marriage. In fact, he presents redemption itself through the analogy of spousal love and sexual union.

According to the analogy, the wife images the church and the husband images Christ. The analogy obviously breaks down (e.g., no husband perfectly images Christ, nor does any wife perfectly image the "spotless bride" of Christ), yet it speaks volumes not only about Christ's spousal love for us but also about the very essence and meaning of marriage. We learn that "marriage corresponds to the vocation of Christians only when it mirrors the love that Christ, the Bridegroom, gives to the church, his bride, and which the church . . . seeks to give back to Christ."[15] Apart from this model, marriage can sink quite quickly into a form of oppression, especially for women.

Again, Paul uses the language of his day but injects it with an entirely new, redemptive meaning. When we understand the nature of the analogy he is using, it makes sense for him to say, "Wives, submit to your husbands *as you do to the Lord*" (v. 22). One way I explain submission in this context is, "Wives, put yourself *under* (sub) the *mission* of your husband." What's the mission of the husband? "Husbands, love your wives, *just as Christ loved the church*." How did Christ love the church? He "gave himself up for her" (v. 25)—unto death! Christ said that he came not to *be* served but *to* serve, to lay down his life for his bride (see Matt. 20:28).

Headship Is a Call to Serve

Perhaps our quickness to accuse Paul of justifying male domination says more about our hang-ups than his. Based on what we've unfolded, when Paul writes, "Wives, submit to your husbands," he is saying, "Wives, allow your husbands to *serve you . . . unto death.*" Wow. The typical interpretation of Paul's words is flipped upside down! Not that the wife is the master and the husband a slave. Power, control, domination—these are the wrong paradigms altogether. Christian marriage calls husband and wife to a *mutual service.* Yet, according to the nature of sexual difference, each lives out this service in different, complementary ways.

If Ephesians says that "the husband is the head of the wife as Christ is the head of the church," this means the husband must be *the first to serve* (see Luke 22:25–26). There is a sacred order to love. In imaging Christ and the church, "the husband is above all *he who loves*, and the wife, on the other hand is *she who is loved*." Thus we can conclude that "the wife's 'submission' to the husband . . . means above all 'the experiencing of love.' This is all the more so, because this 'submission' refers to the image of the submission of the church to Christ, which certainly consists in experiencing his love."[16]

Husbands can and should apply this attitude of being "first to serve" in all areas of married life. But what might it look like in the marriage bed? John Paul II wrote that if a husband is truly to love his wife, "it is necessary to insist that intercourse must not serve merely as a means of allowing [his] climax. . . . The man must take [the] difference between male and female reactions into account . . . so that climax may be reached [by] both . . . and as far as possible occur in both simultaneously." The husband must do this "not for hedonistic, but for altruistic reasons." In this case, if "we take into account the shorter and more violent curve of arousal in the man, [such] tenderness on his part in the context of marital intercourse acquires the significance of an act of virtue."[17]

Mutual climax is not always possible for a whole host of understandable reasons, but we all know the stereotypical image of the selfish husband who takes his pleasure and then rolls over and falls asleep. Such a man cannot be said to love his wife "as Christ loves the church." Christ wants his bride to receive and remain in the fullness of his love so that his joy may be in her and her joy may be complete (see John 15:9–11). And yes, marital intercourse is meant to be an expression and experience of this joy!

The Journey toward Healing

History attests that few men have allowed Paul's words to challenge their selfish inclinations to lust and domination. Instead, we've often used his words to justify our sinful attitudes and behavior. Of course, it's a two-way street. History also demonstrates that women know how to use and manipulate men just as much as men know how to use and manipulate women. That said, women have suffered in a particular way throughout history at the hands of male lust and domination; and, as we mentioned earlier, men seem to have a special responsibility to restore the proper balance of love between the sexes.

How do we begin the long journey toward healing? Christ calls us first and foremost to repentance. In that light, I would like to ask all the women reading this book to allow me, as a representative of the male side of the human race, to apologize humbly for the way male lust and domination have wounded you. The wounds go so very deep in a woman's soul, and I am very, very sorry.

For the ways we have treated you as objects for our own pleasure and enjoyment, please forgive us.

For the ways we have ignored you or rejected you because you haven't met our impossible standards of "beauty," please forgive us.

For the ways we have seen your differences as a threat to our own fragile sense of security rather than as a complement and a gift, please forgive us.

For the ways we have used our strength to manipulate and control you rather than honor and serve you, please forgive us.

For the pride and sense of superiority that have led us to ignore your counsel and belittle your point of view, please forgive us.

In all the ways we have failed to love you as Christ loves the church, please forgive us. We know not what we do.

Jesus, please lead us to the fullness of healing.

Restoration of Holiness

Recall that every married couple has "run out of wine." Spouses who commit themselves to Paul's vision of marriage—properly understood—find that, through all the trials and difficulties of married life, God's grace restores the wine in superabundance. Uniting all of their sorrows and sufferings with those of Christ in his crucifixion, spouses also come to experience the joy of Christ's resurrection. In this way, spouses come to experience their love for each other as something beautifully healing and redemptive.

There is only one Creator. And yet, as we learn in the first pages of Genesis, God shares his creative power with spouses, enabling them to bring new human life into the world. Similarly, there is only one Redeemer. And yet, as we learn in Ephesians 5, God shares his redeeming power with spouses, enabling them to bring new life in Christ to each other. In this way, when spouses love each other with the love of Christ, marital love becomes "redeeming, saving love, the love with which man has been loved by God from eternity in Christ."[18]

Even here on earth, the grace of Christ's spousal love begins restoring in us something of the holiness experienced by the first married couple. "Christ loved the church and gave himself up for her to make her holy" (Eph. 5:25–26). But, as we all know, holiness is not something automatic. In all our trials and struggles, we must continually open ourselves like a bride to receive the gift of Christ's love, allowing it to *in*form and *trans*form us. For holiness "is measured according to the '[profound] mystery' in which the bride responds with the gift of love to the gift of the Bridegroom."[19] Here "the bride" refers to all of us (male and female) in relation to Christ the Bridegroom.

Holiness, then, is not first a matter of *doing* but of *letting it be done to us* (see Luke 1:38). We must allow Christ to put to death all of our disordered ways of relating. We must allow him to sanctify us (make us holy) "by the washing with water through the word" (Eph. 5:26). Scripture scholars see in this a reference to baptism. It was customary in Paul's day for the bride to precede her wedding with a cleansing bath in preparation for her bridegroom. This led the early church to describe baptism itself as the "nuptial bath" that prepares the bride (the church) for communion with Christ. We can see an allusion also to the Lord's Supper when Paul speaks of the nourishment Christ offers his bride (see v. 29).

Chosen in Christ from the Beginning

Just as God organically inscribed the marital union of Adam and Eve in the mystery of creation, he organically inscribes the marital union of the new Adam and the new Eve (Christ and the church) in the mystery of redemption. Spousal union, in fact, becomes the foundation upon which God constructs the entire mystery of our redemption in Christ.[20] The mystery of redemption "clothes itself, so to speak, in the figure and form of the primordial sacrament [marriage]. To the marriage of the first husband and wife . . . corresponds the marriage, or rather the analogy of marriage, of Christ with the church."[21]

Here, in the "spousal character" of both creation and redemption, we recognize an essential continuity regarding God's plan for humanity. We tend to think of Christ's coming as plan B, necessitated when man and woman's sin supposedly thwarted plan A. Our need of redemption from sin certainly flows from the reality of our fall. Yet God's plan for us to share in his own eternal exchange of love remains the same yesterday, today, and forever. Sin, you might say, caused a detour in the fulfillment of that plan, but it didn't thwart it. God's plan for man continues despite sin. "But the plans of the LORD stand firm forever" (Ps. 33:11). That plan—forever and for always—is that all things would be taken up and united in Christ (see Eph. 1:10).

John Paul II cannot stress enough that Christ—the incarnate Christ—has always been at the center of God's plan for man and for the universe. "The Redeemer of man, Jesus Christ, is the centre of the universe and of history."[22] God destined us for union with Christ not only after sin and not only to redeem us from sin. God "chose us in [Christ] before the creation of the world" (Eph. 1:4). *This* is the divine gift that marriage communicates to the world; *this* is the "story" the body tells: we've been chosen in Christ to be united with God forever in an eternal (marital) covenant!

This means that the grace of original innocence (recall the experiences of original solitude, unity, and nakedness) "was granted in consideration of [Christ], . . . although—according to the dimensions of time and history—it preceded the Incarnation."[23] In other words, the love (grace) man and woman knew "in the beginning" through their bodies was a foretaste or preview in some sense of the love (grace) that Christ would pour out within history through his body. In fact, the love that the first couple knew in their bodies *depended* in some sense on the love that Christ would pour out on his bride, the church. Creation foreshadows and prepares us for redemption; the union of the first Adam and Eve foreshadows and prepares us for the union of the new Adam and Eve, Christ and the church.

Again, although it often demands a rethinking of commonly held perceptions, the Bible reveals that the incarnation is not an afterthought in God's mind. We can conclude this because Paul links the one-flesh union of Genesis with the union of Christ and the church. "'For this reason a man will leave his father and mother and be united to his wife, and the two will become one flesh.' This is a profound mystery—but I am talking about Christ and the church" (Eph. 5:31–32). Right from the beginning—before sin—conjugal union foreshadowed the incarnation, Christ's union with humanity in one flesh. We've been called to this eternal union "not because of anything we have done but because of his own purpose and grace." And, as the apostle Paul himself affirms, "This grace was given us in Christ Jesus before the beginning of time" (2 Tim. 1:9).

This Is a "Profound Mystery"

The apostle's linking of the one-flesh union with the union of Christ and the church "is the most important point of the whole text, *in some sense its keystone*."[24] Both "the union of Christ with the church and the spousal union of man and woman in marriage are in this way illuminated by a particular supernatural light."[25]

Guided by this supernatural light, Paul demonstrates a keen understanding of the sacramentality of the body. The body is a sacrament in the sense that it makes visible the invisible. In examining Ephesians 5, John Paul II recalls his thesis: "The body, in fact, and only the body, is capable of making visible what is invisible: the spiritual and divine. It has been created to transfer into the visible reality of the world the mystery hidden from eternity in God, and thus to be a sign of it."[26]

Recall what we mean by "the mystery hidden from eternity in God": (1) God is a communion of love and (2) we are destined to share in that exchange through our union with Christ. The sacrament consists in manifesting that mystery in a sign that both proclaims the mystery and enables us to share in it.[27] The author of Ephesians speaks of two signs—one from the order of creation and the other from the order of redemption—that communicate God's mystery of love.

In creation, God's mystery of love "became a *visible reality through the union* of the first man and woman" (see Gen. 2:24). In redemption, that same mystery of divine love becomes "*a visible reality in the indissoluble union of Christ with the church*, which the author of Ephesians presents as the spousal union."[28] With regard to these signs, these two unions, we are speaking "in reference to the entire work of creation and redemption."[29] The marriage of the first Adam and Eve is a sign of the entire work of creation, and the marriage of the new Adam and Eve (Christ and the church) is a sign of the entire work of redemption.

The Meaning of Human Life

John Paul II remarks that it is a particular merit of the apostle Paul that he brought these two signs (the one-flesh union and the union of Christ and the church) together, making of them *the single profound sign*, that is, *a profound sacrament*.[30] Through this profound sacrament the "profound mystery" of human life is revealed.

The linking of these two unions is obviously important "to the Christian vocation of husbands and wives." However, it "is equally essential and valid *for the [understanding] of man* in general: for the fundamental problem of understanding him and for the self-understanding of his being in the world." Indeed, it is in this link that we "find the answer to the question about the meaning of 'being a body.'"[31]

What is that meaning? We are called to love as Christ loves. This is the new commandment Christ gives us: "Love each other as I have loved you" (John 15:12). How did Christ love us? "This is my body . . . given for you" (Luke 22:19). With these words spoken at the Last Supper, Christ not only shows us the meaning of love. Through his death and resurrection, his body also empowers us to love others in the same way and to recognize that this is the "story" our bodies tell.

Remember the tears of my father-in-law when he received communion for the first time after consummating his marriage? My father-in-law realized that day that the meaning of life, the meaning of the universe, is inscribed not only in our souls but also in our bodies—in the "profound mystery" of sexual difference and our call to become one flesh. As we will see even more clearly in the next chapter, spousal union is the "great sign" that God has given to the world to reveal the mystery of his own love.

SIX

SEX REFERS TO CHRIST AND HIS CHURCH

[The love of man and woman] is a clue to a deeper reality. . . .
For this exotic intimacy was given to us as a picture of something else, something truly out of this world.

—John Eldredge

As you may have guessed, I never wrote that book—*Loving Her Rightly*. If I ever do, I imagine it will be coauthored by Wendy West.

Perhaps chief among the lessons that my marriage continues to teach me is that I don't need to hide my faults, sins, and weaknesses in order to be loveable. Somehow, I had absorbed a very different message growing up, and it created a rather crippling perfectionism in my life from which I'm still recovering, long into adulthood.

It seems that many people think that a saint is someone who has it all together, and so that's what we strive for. But the only

113

way to "accomplish" that is to bury all of our brokenness and pretend it isn't there. Since the dawn of original sin, we've been hiding from God (and one another) out of fear that we're not loveable. Faith in God's love casts this fear out (see 1 John 4:18), enabling us to bring all of our brokenness into the light, knowing we will not be chided or condemned but embraced, forgiven, healed. "I was afraid because I was naked; so I hid [myself]" (Gen. 3:10) is transformed into "I was at peace because I know God loves me; so I exposed myself."

This is the kind of love that spouses are meant to share with one another: the love that allows them to be "naked without shame"—to "see and know each other . . . with all the peace of the interior gaze."[1] As we know well, it's at the deepest spiritual level of our humanity—not merely the physical level— that we're afraid of our "nakedness" and, thus, find ourselves hiding. True love, however, is not afraid of the other person's warts. In fact, the strength of such a love emerges most clearly when the beloved person stumbles, when his or her weaknesses or even sins come into the open. One who truly loves does not then withdraw his love, but loves all the more, loves in full consciousness of the other's shortcomings and faults. For the person as such never loses his or her essential value.[2]

Becoming a Human Sign of Divine Love

As we will learn more clearly in this chapter, the indispensable path to learning how to love in this healing, redemptive way is learning how to pray in this healing, redemptive way. As the parable of the tax collector and the Pharisee who went to the temple to pray shows us, the self-righteous put masks on when they pray. Repentant sinners who trust in God's love take them off (see Luke 18:9–14). In true, intimate prayer, we let the Lord love us as we really are, and we let that love purify us so that we can become who we are meant to be. In turn, by receiving the *divine love* by which we are loved, we can become *human signs* of that love to others. And that is what marriage is all about.

We have already said much about the nature of marital love as a sign of God's love. In this chapter, John Paul II's teaching will help us get even more specific. We will first explore the idea that the body has a God-given "language." We will then look at two examples of married couples who speak that language truthfully. The lovers in the Song of Songs are the first couple. Tobias and Sarah from the ancient book of Tobit are the second.[3] Each couple can help us understand different dimensions of the "sign language" of married love.

The "Sign Language" of Marriage

From the outset of this book, we've discussed the fact that God speaks to us in sign language. All of creation—not just as a whole but each bird, each blade of grass, each star in the sky, and so on—is a sign from God that speaks to us (if we have ears to hear, that is). If you're not accustomed to seeing creation this way, "ask the animals, and they will teach you, or the birds in the sky, and they will tell you; or speak to the earth, and it will teach you, or let the fish of the sea inform you" (Job 12:7–8). What will they tell you? All of creation proclaims that God is life-giving love! As I wrote in *Fill These Hearts*:

> If God is speaking to us through the natural world, then it's clear that one of his favorite subjects is mating and fertility, coupling and life-givingness. One has to be blind not to recognize this unending "song" of love and life everywhere. . . . Listen, and you will hear all of nature singing its own version

115

of the Song of Songs, that biblical "ode to eros" that whispers the secrets of divine love. And nature's song culminates in *us*—in the "theology" of our bodies. Our bodies tell the story of divine love. It's written into the very design of our masculinity and femininity.[4]

What is it about masculinity and femininity that tells the story of God's life-giving love if not the call of the two to be "fruitful and increase in number" (Gen. 1:28)? "That is why a man leaves his father and mother and is united to his wife, and they become one flesh" (Gen. 2:24). *What* is the reason? The apostle Paul tells us: to signify (become a sign of) the "mystery, which for ages past was kept hidden in God" (Eph. 3:9) but has now been revealed in Christ and his love for the church (see Eph. 5:31–32).

Christian marriage is the commitment to *be* this sign to the world—to become more and more a true image of Christ's love for the church. This, in fact, is what traditional Christian wedding vows express: the commitment to love "as Christ loves the church." But this is not only a commitment of the will and of the heart. If wedding vows express a language of the heart—a language of the *spirit*—there must be a corresponding language of the *body*.

The Language of the Body

We all know that we can speak through the language of our bodies without uttering a word. A wave of the hand says hello or goodbye. A shrug of the shoulders says, "I don't know." A raised fist expresses anger.

The body also speaks an amazingly profound language in sexual intercourse. "Through gestures and reactions, through the whole . . . dynamism of tension and enjoyment—whose direct source is the body in its masculinity and femininity, the body in its action and interaction—through all this *man, the person,* 'speaks.' . . . Precisely on the level of this 'language of the body' . . . man and woman reciprocally express *themselves* in the fullest and most profound way made possible for them by . . . their masculinity and femininity."[5]

But what is sexual intercourse meant to express? What is its true language, its true meaning? As the Bible shows us in Ephesians 5, the bodily union of a man and a woman is meant to express divine love. Precisely here, in the consummation of their marriage, spouses are meant to participate in the fullest way in the "profound mystery" of Christ's union with the church (see Eph. 5:31–32). Whether they realize it or not, this is the power of the language of their bodies. Sexual intercourse is sacramental: it's a visible sign of a spiritual and divine reality.

But if erotic love is meant to express the language of agape, we must properly understand this language. Christ's love seems distinguishable by four particular qualities. First, Christ gives his body *freely* ("No one takes [my life] from me, but I lay it down of my own accord," John 10:18). Second, he gives his body *totally*—without reservation, condition, or selfish calculation ("He loved them to the end," John 13:1). Third, he gives his body *faithfully* ("I am with you always," Matt. 28:20). And fourth, he gives his body *fruitfully* ("I have come that they may have life," John 10:10). If men and women are to avoid the pitfalls of counterfeit love and live their vocation to the full, their union must strive to express the same *free, total, faithful, fruitful* love that Christ's body expresses.

Another name for this kind of love is *marriage.* This is precisely what a bride and groom commit to in Christian marriage. As part of the traditional Christian wedding ceremony, the minister asks the couple: "Have you come here *freely* and *without reservation* to give yourselves to each other in marriage? Do you promise to be *faithful* all the days of your lives? Do you promise to *receive children* lovingly from God?" The bride and groom each say yes.

In turn, spouses are meant to express this same yes *with their bodies* whenever they become one flesh. "In fact, the words themselves, 'I take you as my wife / as my husband' can only be fulfilled by conjugal intercourse."[6] With conjugal intercourse, "we pass *to the reality* that corresponds to these words." Both the words of the wedding vows and the act of conjugal intercourse "are important *with regard to the structure of the sacramental sign.*"[7] Intercourse, then, is where the words of the wedding vows *become flesh*. It's where men and women are meant to *incarnate* divine love. It's a fine thing when a couple returns to the church to renew their vows on a special anniversary, but this shouldn't undermine the fact that every time a husband and wife have intercourse, they are meant to renew their wedding vows with the language of their bodies.

"The Bible is full of covenant renewal ceremonies," writes Tim Keller. "The ultimate covenant renewal ceremony is the Lord's Supper." Here we "reenact the total commitment and oneness we have in Christ as a way of renewing and deepening that oneness." In the same way, sexual union "is a covenant renewal ceremony for marriage, the physical reenactment of the inseparable oneness in all other areas—economic, legal, personal, psychological—created by the marriage covenant. Sex renews and revitalizes the marriage covenant."[8]

The Christian sexual ethic begins to make perfect and beautiful sense when viewed through this lens. It's not a prudish list of prohibitions. It's a call to embrace our own "greatness," our own God-given dignity. It's a call to live the love we're created for, the love we so ardently desire.

Distinguishing True and False Prophets

John Paul II goes so far as to describe the body and sexual union as "prophetic." A prophet is someone who speaks for God, who proclaims his mystery. This is what the marital embrace is meant to proclaim. But we must be careful, of course, to distinguish true and false prophets.[9] If we can speak the truth with our bodies, we can also speak lies.

We all know it is possible to lie with our bodies. Suppose a used-car salesman knowingly sells you a lemon and then shakes your hand. Didn't he just lie with his body? What about the kiss of Judas? It was a lie. And who do you think prompts us to lie with our bodies? The father of lies is hell-bent on getting us to speak his own language with our bodies. Why? To keep us from the "profound mystery" of Christ's union with the church—that is, to keep us from eternal life.

Recall that the battle for man's soul is fought over the truth of his body. If the body is meant to sing the greatest of all songs—the Song of Songs—we must be well aware that there is an enemy who hates the divine-human harmony of this song and eagerly wants to insert his own sour notes. If God designed the body to be a sign of his own love and life, the enemy wants to counter that sign with lust and death. This is why when spouses "unite as husband and wife, they . . . find themselves in the situation in which *the powers of good and evil fight against each other*." Their choices and acts, in fact, "take on the whole weight of human existence in the union of the two."[10]

How, then, in the midst of such a sobering battle, can men and women be sure that love and life will win? John Paul II turns to the lovers of the Song of Songs and the marriage of Tobias and Sarah as two shining examples of the triumph of love and life over lust and death.

The Agony and the Ecstasy

Since marriage is a sign of Christ's love for the church, spouses can expect throughout their married life to experience both the agony of the cross and the ecstasy of the resurrection. If the Song of Songs reveals the *ecstasy* of becoming one flesh, the marriage of Tobias and Sarah reveals the *agony*. Only by holding the two together do we get a realistic vision of marriage.

In an article entitled "Divorce: In the Image and Likeness of Hell," Melinda Selmys speaks plainly of her frustration with the sweet, pious lingo with which many Christians often speak about marriage. "The theologians remind us that our married life is an image of the union between . . . Christ [and the church]. We hear of . . . the bliss of the two becoming one." When things get tough, we are told "to improve our communication, fall in love with each other all over again, observe the tender moments, etc., etc."

Then she allows such platitudes to butt up against the all-too-real experiences of actual marriages. "But how are you to fall in love again," she asks, "with an insensitive beast who has broken your heart and slept with another woman? How can you see your sex life as an image of the intimate life of the blessed Trinity when your wife consents only on a full moon when Mars is in Virgo, and makes love with the enthusiasm of a dead frog?"[11] I didn't know whether to laugh or cry the first time I read that last line. For whatever reason, such brutally honest writing seems rare in much of the Christian world. It's as if those who promote biblical teaching on marriage are afraid it won't go over so well if we talk about the real sufferings of following Jesus. So we conveniently promote the glories of the Christian life without a realistic assessment of the sorrows.

Marriage is a messy, painful business. If spouses are to love as Christ loves, how could it be otherwise? Christ's marriage is consummated *through his passion and death*. This means, as Selmys observes, that marriage will involve "the same agony, the mingling of tears and blood, the same thorns digging into our skulls, the same nails plowed through our palms." In light of how many people believe Christianity is disparaging of sex, the glories and ecstasies to which authentic biblical teaching calls spouses (as exemplified in the Song of Songs) *should* be emphasized. But these glories and ecstasies are the fruit of embracing *much* purifying suffering (as exemplified in the marriage of Tobias and Sarah). If the joy is not set before us, we will have no motivation to endure the suffering: it was "for the joy set before him [that Christ] endured the cross" (Heb. 12:2). But if the path to those joys is not also realistically assessed, we will naively wonder why marriage can be so difficult, even agonizing.

Holding the two together—the agony and the ecstasy—gives us the proper picture. A picture of the ecstasy emerges first as we look at the Song of Songs.

The Biblical Ode to Erotic Love

The Song of Songs "is filled with barefaced rejoicing in sexual pleasure," writes Tim Keller. As such, he observes that it "can be very uncomfortable for the prudish."[12] Why, we must ask, is this unabashed celebration of erotic love the favorite biblical book of so many of the greatest saints and theologians of Christian history? What do they know that we need to get in on?

Gregory of Nyssa, one of the greatest minds of the early church, provides the answer when he observes that human nature "can neither discover nor entertain anything greater" than "the mystery contained in the Song of Songs." The superlative nature of the title itself tells us that Christ "promises to teach us mysteries of mysteries by the agency of the Song of Songs." And that agency, Gregory reminds us, is "the passion of erotic love." This "most intense of pleasurable activities . . . is set as a figure at the very fore of the guidance that the teachings give so that we may learn that it is necessary for the soul [to] . . . boil with love . . . heated by that 'fire' which the Lord came to 'cast upon the earth' (Luke 12:49)."[13]

As we've pondered throughout this book, God's eternal plan is to marry us—to live with us in an eternal union of love that the Bible compares to the union of spouses in one flesh. The Song of Songs takes us to the very heart of biblical faith. And that heart is this: we can enter into nuptial union with God, our deepest aspiration. The erotic love poetry of the Song of Songs gives us entrance to the wedding feast that never ends. It transposes heaven's love song into an earthly key, enabling us to hit the notes, so to speak.

Yet the Song of Songs is not merely an allegory of God's "spiritual" love. A growing number of biblical scholars maintain that the Song of Songs is "to be taken simply as what it manifestly is: a song of human love." For "human love, created and blessed by God, can be the theme of an inspired biblical book."[14] John Paul II seems to agree with the view of Luis Alonso Schökel that those who have "forgotten the lovers" or "petrified them into pretense" have not interpreted the Song correctly. "He who does not believe in the human love of the spouses, he who must ask forgiveness for the body, does not have the right to rise higher. . . . With the affirmation of human love, by contrast, it is possible to discover the revelation of God in it."[15]

This confirms an essential element of incarnational reality. Grace—the mystery of God's life and covenant love—is communicated *through* the "stuff" of our humanity, not despite it. The "content of the Song of Songs is at the same time sexual and sacred." When we ignore the sacred, we see the Song merely as a secular erotic poem. But when we ignore the sexual, we fall into *allegorism*—that is, we ignore the physical and sensual reality of the lovers. "It is only by putting these two aspects together that one can read the book in the right way."[16]

Recall that our goal in this chapter is to reflect on the human dimension of marriage as a physical sign of God's life and love. This is precisely what the erotic poetry of the Song of Songs helps us do.

The Bride as "Sister"

Interestingly, the lover in the Song repeatedly refers to his beloved as "sister" *before* calling her "bride." "You have stolen my heart, my sister, my bride; you have stolen my heart with one glance of your eyes. . . . How delightful is your love, my sister, my bride!" (Song 4:9–10). These words are "impregnated," John Paul II says, "with a particular content."[17] It is as if the lovers in the Song had "descended from the same family circle, as though from infancy they had been united by memories of the common hearth. In this way, they reciprocally feel as close as brother and sister who owe their existence to the same mother."[18]

Authentic marital love always recognizes one's spouse as a brother or sister who shares the same humanity. Both male and female are made in the image and likeness of God. In this way, recognizing his beloved first as "sister" echoes Adam's words, "This is now bone of my bones and flesh of my flesh" (Gen. 2:23).

While the idea of being recognized first as a "sister" usually brings great relief to the woman, it can present a certain challenge for the man. More specifically, it challenges him to assess his motives. Is he motivated by the passion of love or by the egoism of lust, by the sincere gift of self or merely by a desire to gratify himself? The normal man recoils at the idea of lusting after his sister—*and so should a man recoil at the thought of lusting after his bride*! This is precisely the point. The lover of the Song accepts this challenge and does not hesitate to call his beloved "sister." With such a recognition, he demonstrates that his desire for her as "bride" is not one of lust but of love. With *"a disinterested tenderness,"*[19] the lover desires only to be a sincere gift to his beloved according to the image of God.

Lest there be any doubt, let's be certain here that such disinterested tenderness does not dampen the passion and pleasure of love; it rather intensifies it. Purity in love is all about restoring the original fullness of God's plan for man and woman. As C. S. Lewis reminds us, "The old Christian teachers said that if man had never fallen, sexual pleasure, instead of being less than it is now, would actually have been greater."[20] This certainly seems to be the experience of the lovers in the Song of Songs.

Garden Closed, Fountain Sealed

The groom demonstrates the genuine character of his love all the more when he says, "You are a garden locked up, my sister, my bride; you are a spring enclosed, a sealed fountain" (Song 4:12). These metaphors remain in a very strict relation with the one-flesh union and thus help us to understand its mystery, especially the mystery of the woman. We can see the great value of these expressions in their ability to convey the profoundly personal dimension and meaning of the union of the lovers. "The language of metaphors—poetic language—seems to be especially appropriate and precise in this sphere."[21]

Both of these metaphors—"garden locked" and "fountain sealed"—express the whole personal dignity of the female sex. They speak with profound reverence for the mystery of the feminine body and, since the body expresses the person, of the feminine personality. These expressions indicate that the "bride *presents herself to the eyes of the man as the master of her own mystery*."[22] The groom must—and in the Song of Songs does—respect the fact that he cannot master his bride: he cannot, must not, dominate or control her. She is in control of her own person, her own "mystery." For every human person is an inviolable mystery as a unique reflection of God's own mystery.

The point is that authentic love affords a certain entering into the mystery of the other person without ever violating the mystery of the person.[23] If a person's "love" violates the one loved, then *it is not love* and should not be called love. It is love's counterfeit—lust. If the lover is to enter this garden without violating the woman's mystery, he cannot barge in or break down the door. Nor can he manipulate her into surrendering the key. If he is to respect his wife as "master of her own mystery," all the lover can do is entrust himself to her freedom. All he can do is knock at the garden gate and respectfully await her response.

The lover in the Song initiates the gift, making his desire clear: "Open to me, my sister, my darling, my dove, my flawless one. My head is drenched with dew" (Song 5:2). And she hears him: "Listen! My beloved is knocking" (5:2). But he puts "his hand through the latch" (5:4) only with her freely given yes—a yes given without any hint of being coerced or manipulated. In total freedom, she surrenders to him; she opens her garden to him, making it his: "Awake, north wind, and come, south wind! Blow on my garden, that its fragrance may spread everywhere. Let my beloved come into his garden and taste its choice fruits" (4:16).

Thus, in the course of their dialogue of love, "*the 'garden closed' opens up in some way before the eyes of the bridegroom's soul and body.*"[24] And with profound reverence and awe ("Submit to one another *out of reverence . . .*"), he beholds her mystery unveiled. He comes to her delighting in her gift, remaining ever in awe of her freely opened garden: "I have come into my garden, my sister, my bride; I have gathered my myrrh with my spice. I have eaten my honeycomb and my honey; I have drunk my wine and my milk" (Song 5:1).

These boldly erotic verses reveal the mystery of authentic love. The spouses' ecstatic love provides an "essential sign of holiness."[25] In other words, the spouses in the Song are correctly reading the true language of their bodies as a sign of divine love. Thus the human dimension of their marriage (their human love and sexual union) enables them to share in the divine dimension (God's love and grace).

Set Me as a Seal

Sexual intercourse, as the moment of marital consummation, is the specific moment in which the marriage bond binds the couple together until death. In this way, "the man and the woman together . . . constitute the sign of the reciprocal gift of self, which *sets the seal on their whole life.*"[26] This is the power and meaning of sexual union as God designed it. Sexual intercourse

126

has a language that proclaims, "I am totally yours unto death. I belong to you and you to me until death do us part."

It's not just that sexual union belongs "in" marriage. Rather, it is that sexual union—as God designed it—has an inherently *marital* meaning: it expresses wedding vows. That's why sexual intercourse is called the *marital* embrace. Sex is only what it is meant to be when it expresses a love that is "as strong as death." The bride confirms her knowledge of this when she says, "Place me like a seal over your heart, . . . for love is as strong as death. . . . It burns like blazing fire, like a mighty flame. Many waters cannot quench love; rivers cannot sweep it away" (Song 8:6–7).

John Paul II says that these words bring us to the peak of the Song's declaration of love. They seem to present the final chords of the Song, the "final chords in the 'language of the body.'" When we read that "love is as strong as death," we discover "the closure and crowning of everything in the Song of Songs that begins with the metaphor 'garden closed' and 'fountain sealed.'"[27]

With these words, the lover had presented himself to his beloved not as one superficially attracted to her body. Rather, he presented himself as one who was captivated and fascinated by her entire mystery as a woman, as one ready to uphold the whole personal dignity of her sexuality, as one desirous of honoring her as a feminine person, as a sister and a bride—unto death. Here we see that a woman can open her sacred garden to her lover and remain inviolate only if she is assured that he is ready and willing to commit his *entire life* to her, if she is assured that he has placed her *like a seal over his heart*, if she is assured that his love will be *as strong as death*. The love that is as strong as death is called marriage.

People don't need the Bible to know that sexual love is meant to be permanent. Permanence is what the heart longs for. Turn on the radio and you will hear song after song proclaiming this desire for love that lasts forever. In teaching that sex is meant to express lasting love (that is, marital love), the Bible is simply inviting us to be true to the song that wells up from the deepest recesses of our souls. Listen to it! It's the Song of Songs.

Sexual Union Is a Test of Life or Death

If the lovers in the Song of Songs help us distinguish between authentic love and lust, the marriage of Tobias and Sarah in the ancient book of Tobit[28] demonstrates just what is at stake in this distinction. From the first moment of their marriage, Tobias and Sarah had to face the test of life or death. "The words about love 'strong as death,' spoken by the spouses of the Song of Songs, . . . here take on the character of a real test."[29]

As the story goes, Sarah had already been married seven times, but, because of the work of a demon, each groom died before having intercourse with her (talk about an anticlimactic honeymoon—and seven times in a row! Tob. 6:13–14). Then an angel appears to Tobias and tells him that he is to marry Sarah. John Paul II—man of keen observation that he is—remarks that Tobias had reason to be afraid. In fact, on the day of their wedding, Sarah's father was already digging Tobias's grave (Tob. 8:9)!

Tobias courageously faces the test. He takes Sarah as his wife, enters the bridal chamber—and lives to consummate their marriage. Why does he live? Because "during the test of the first wedding night, *love supported by prayer is revealed as stronger than death*."[30] Love "is victorious because it prays."[31] Take a careful look at Tobias and Sarah's prayer. It contains a short review of everything we have discussed in the TOB.

"Blessed are you, O God . . . and blessed be your holy and glorious name for ever. . . . You made Adam and gave him Eve his wife as a helper and support. You said, 'It is not good that the man should be alone; let us make a helper for him like himself.' And now, O Lord, I am not taking this sister of mine because of lust, but with sincerity. Grant that I may find mercy and grow old together with her." And she said with him, "Amen." (Tob. 8:5–8, my translation)

John Paul II describes this prayer as the spouses' "conjugal creed."[32] This creed originates from the depth of love in the new spouses' hearts and expresses itself in the life-giving language of their bodies. As such, this creed serves as a precise antidote to the demon's plot to write *lust* into their hearts and *death* into their bodies. Tobias first praises God for his sheer goodness. Then, as Christ will direct us to do, he sets his heart on God's original plan for marriage. He calls Sarah "sister" like the lover in the Song of Songs. He contrasts *lust* with the *sincere gift of self*. He knows that he needs God's mercy to live the truth of love, and he longs to spend his whole life with her. Sarah's "Amen" demonstrates that she shares one and the same desire.

Tobias's love for Sarah is a type of Christ's love for the church. Christ stared death in the face on the "marriage bed" of the cross, thus consummating his love for the church and conquering death by rising to new life. Tobias also stared death in the face on his marriage bed, and inspired with sacrificial (Christlike) love, he also conquered death. After seven men had succumbed, Tobias consummates the marriage and lives!

If sexual union is a test of life or death, then in the face of authentic spousal love, death has no chance. "Where, O death, is your victory? Where, O death, is your sting?" (1 Cor. 15:55). Spouses who by God's grace love one another according to

God's original plan—and who trust in God's mercy when they fail to love one another rightly—have no fear of this test. They are ready and willing to place themselves "between the forces of good and evil . . . because love is confident in the victory of good and is ready to do everything in order that good may conquer."[33]

Spousal Love as Prayer

We have already learned much about the "profound mystery" spoken of in Ephesians 5. At the end of his chapter on marriage as a human sign of divine love, John Paul II returns to this classic text to reconfirm even more deeply the profound meaning of joining in one flesh. He observes that if the sacramental sign of marriage is based on the language of the body reread in the truth of love, then Ephesians 5 offers us the definitive expression of this sign reread in the truth of love.

The Song of Songs contains "the language of the body in all the richness of its subjective meaning." In other words, the lovers' duet in the Song allows us in some way to enter their interior, subjective experience of love, as does the story of Tobias and Sarah. Ephesians 5, on the other hand, "contains *the 'objective' confirmation of this language* in its entirety."[34] There we read that the one-flesh union is a "profound mystery" that is meant to express and proclaim the love of Christ and the church. Despite what a given couple might express subjectively, Ephesians 5 presents the objective truth of the language of the body: what it is always *meant* to express.

The internal goal (and lifelong challenge!) of every marriage is for the spouses to ensure that what they express *subjectively* in their sexual union confirms the *objective* truth of God's plan. As countless couples can attest, simply getting married is not enough to make sexual union something holy and beautiful. Marriage is the objective prerequisite to experience the true glory and holiness of sex. But the couple's *ethos*—their inner orientation and desires—must come to correspond to the true dignity of the person and the true meaning of spousal love. This, of course, calls for lifelong conversion and healing. In a word, it demands a life of deep prayer.

Prayer, as we observed earlier, is where we must learn to let our masks fall. It's where we must offer ourselves as we really are to the Lord who loves us, so he can purify and transform us. This is precisely what Tobias and Sarah did before uniting— from within the bridal chamber, they sought the Lord in prayer: "'And now, O Lord, I am not taking this sister of mine because of lust, but with sincerity. Grant that I may find mercy.'... And she said with him, 'Amen'" (Tob. 8:7–8 RSV). Here we witness the moment of purification to which spouses must submit themselves if they wish to express the spousal meaning of the body in all its truth.

To the degree that this profound integration between objective reality and subjective experience occurs, spouses experience the language of the body for what it is: they experience it as *the language of the liturgy*.[35] This idea brings us to the pinnacle of the value of spousal love. Here we cross the threshold of the "profound mystery" and enter into the deepest integration of the sexual and the sacred.

In some Christian circles today, "liturgy" has gotten a bad name. For the ancients, liturgy meant the participation of the people of God in the work of God. The work of God refers above all to the "profound mystery" of our redemption in Christ accomplished through his death and resurrection. To say that spousal love is "liturgical" is to say that it participates in this "profound mystery." The cross is where Christ consummated his marriage. Hence, spouses are "the permanent reminder to the church of what happened on the cross."[36]

Liturgy is also the church's celebration of divine worship. When lived according to the "profound mystery" of God's designs, the marital embrace itself becomes a profound prayer. It becomes "eucharistic"—an act of thanksgiving offered to God for the joyous gift of sharing in his life and love (the Greek word *eucharistia* means "thanksgiving"). According to the analogy, we might even view the marital bed as an altar upon which spouses offer their bodies in living sacrifice, holy and acceptable to God. This is their spiritual act of worship (see Rom. 12:1).

If the sexual revolution of the twentieth century turned sex into an idol to be worshiped, the Christian revolution, as I say in my book *Heaven's Song*, "transforms sex from something that is *worshiped* to something that is *worship*."[37]

Prayer as Nuptial Union

Such a lofty vision of marital intercourse may seem hopelessly unrealistic, even undesirable to some: "Come on—sex is meant to be a prayer? Like my husband would ever go for that!" Or, "Who wants sex to be prayerful? What a turnoff!"

While it may be the case that a given spouse has no interest in pursuing a "prayerful sex life," the above sentiments reflect tragically misinformed notions of both sex and prayer. Regarding prayer as a turnoff, authentic prayer does turn off lust. But authentic prayer turns on the noble and deep-flowing passion of genuine eros. In fact, the greatest saints and theologians of Christian history—from Augustine and John Chrysostom to Teresa of Ávila and John of the Cross—can find no better language with which to describe prayer itself than the language of erotic love.

Prayer, from this perspective, is akin to the surrender of the bride to her bridegroom. If we are to take the spousal analogy of the Bible with the seriousness it deserves, we must recognize that when we pray, we are seeking union with the Lord: spousal union, nuptial union. This means that we must have the courage to "get naked" before God (remove the fig leaves / take our masks off) so that the heavenly Bridegroom can enter our hearts and love us *freely*, *totally*, *faithfully*, and *fruitfully*. "According to the words of Sacred Scripture," writes John Paul II, "God penetrates the creature, who is completely 'naked' before him."[38]

What we are learning in the TOB is that only to the degree that we are living in nuptial union with God are we capable of living in authentic nuptial union with an earthly spouse. This is what joining in one flesh is: a sacramental sign of union with God. Could there possibly be a more exalted notion of sexual union than to see it as a sign of union with God?

Imaging God's Love

If the lovers of the Song of Songs proclaim the joy of living the true sign of marital love, while Tobias and Sarah face a test of life or death to reclaim the truth of that sign, what light does this shed on the biblical vision of sexual morality?

Ultimately, from an authentic biblical perspective, all questions of sexual morality come down to one very simple question: Does what we're doing with our bodies image God's *free*, *total*, *faithful*, *fruitful* love, or does it miss the mark? If it misses the mark, is the solution to adjust the target or to adjust our aim?

Think of it this way: If sexual intercourse is meant to be a renewal of wedding vows, how healthy would a marriage be if spouses were regularly unfaithful to their vows? On the other

133

hand, how healthy would a marriage be if spouses regularly renewed their vows, expressing an ever-increasing commitment to them? As we will see more clearly in the next chapter, this is precisely what is at stake in questions of sexual morality.

But it's not up to us to try really hard to love as God loves. *We simply cannot do it.* Our job, rather, is to open to the gift of his love that he wants to pour into our hearts. "God's love has been poured out into our hearts through the Holy Spirit, who has been given to us" (Rom. 5:5). A life of deep prayer and union with the Holy Spirit—this is what opens us to the divine gift of love, like a bride opening to the gift of her bridegroom. Continually receiving so great a gift, we are enabled to share that love with others. This is the only context in which we can properly understand the authentically Christian vision of sexual morality.

SEVEN

KEEPING GOD IN THE BEDROOM

> One of the ends for which sex was created was to symbolize to us the hidden things of God. . . . We have no authority to take the living and seminal figures which God has painted on the canvas of our nature and shift them about as if they were mere geometrical figures.
>
> —C. S. Lewis

The above statement from Lewis is in deep agreement with the biblical study we've been undertaking. Indeed, what we've been unfolding throughout this book is precisely how sex symbolizes "the hidden things of God" and what those hidden things are. In this chapter, we'll unfold the implications of Lewis's other sentence: What happens when we take "the living and seminal figures which God has painted on the canvas of our nature" as male and female and "shift them about as if they were mere geometrical figures"?

Perhaps at this point you're feeling some trepidation. You're beginning to understand the biblical logic we've unfolded, you can see where it's headed, and you know your life doesn't measure up. Welcome to the human race. The good news is that Christ can restore us to the full measure of our humanity. Remember from our discussion in chapter 3 that Christ has come to save the world, beginning with eros. There is new wine poured out for us. We need only open our hearts to this wine and allow it in to do its healing, transforming work. It doesn't matter where you've been or what mistakes you've made. The authentic biblical vision of sexuality is a message of salvation, not condemnation.

Embracing Our "Greatness"

Authentic Christian morality is not against us. It's unstintingly *for* us. It's nothing but a call to embrace our own "greatness," our own true dignity. This is what our study of God's Word has been revealing all along—our dignity, our greatness as male and female. This dignity and greatness rests above all on the fact that men and women are both made in the image of God and called to communion with God. And that is what their communion is meant to signify. The union of husband and wife in one flesh is the sacrament or sign of God's eternal mystery of life-giving love and communion and our call to share in that eternal bliss through communion with Christ. Now it's time to follow these stupendous truths to their logical conclusion.

At the close of the previous chapter, I observed that all questions of sexual morality ultimately come down to one: Does what we're doing with our bodies truly signify God's *free, total, faithful, fruitful* love, or does it miss the mark? My book *Good News about Sex and Marriage* uses this principle to answer 140 of the most common questions on the subject. I refer you to that for a more detailed discussion. For now we'll just apply the principle to a few specific questions, with the aim of arriving at the core of sexual morality.

Before we do, however, it's critical that we hold God's hands of mercy. Without grounding ourselves there, we will be tempted either to despair over our sin or to rationalize it away. If God's mercy and forgiveness are real, we should never fear to acknowledge where we have missed the mark. The only sin we should fear, in fact, is the rationalization of sin—the refusal to acknowledge sin as sin. Such obstinacy involves the blaspheming of the Holy Spirit that Jesus referred to as the unforgivable sin (see Matt. 12:32). It's unforgivable because it's unrepentant. So if we discover that we have "missed the mark," let us be repentant, and let us entrust ourselves to God's mercy. Only from that secure place can we look honestly at sin without despairing or rationalizing. Here we go.

Does an act of masturbation image God's *free, total, faithful, fruitful* love, or does it miss the mark? Does an act of fornication (sex between two unmarried people) image God's *free, total, faithful, fruitful* love, or does it miss the mark? What about an act of adultery? What about homosexual behavior? What about lusting after pornographic images? What about treating one's spouse as an object for one's own selfish gratification?

To recognize the incompatibility of these behaviors with living in the image of God is not to condemn those who might engage in such behaviors. Once again, Christ came not to condemn; he came to *save*. The truth, although it can sting, sets us free. That's the goal: to embrace the truth that allows us to live in the freedom for which Christ has set us free!

Orienting Sex toward the Eternal

Tragically, lies about our sexuality are in style in today's world, and Christians themselves, in the name of being relevant, have been buying into them on a large scale. Pastor Rick Warren offers a powerful and sobering challenge to believers in this regard: "Just because a lie is popular doesn't make it the truth. Just because something wrong is popular doesn't make it right. Just because something evil is popular doesn't make it good. We have to realize that truth is always true and we build our lives on this foundation. If you build your life on what's in style, here's the problem: everything that's in style inevitably goes out of style. . . . *The only way to be relevant is to be eternal.*"[1]

To be relevant with regard to our sexuality is to recognize its eternal meaning and its eternal orientation. "Sexual orientation" has become quite a buzzword in today's world, and it means a host of things to a host of people. But as we've been learning throughout this Bible study, the most fundamental sexual orientation there is—its God-given orientation—is orientation toward the eternal, toward the marriage of Christ and the church.

"*This* is the deepest meaning [and] most profound purpose of marriage," explains Rick Warren. "And this is the strongest reason why marriage can only be between a man and a woman. There is no other relationship—including the parent-child relationship—that can picture this intimate union. To redefine marriage," Warren concludes, "would destroy the picture that God intends for marriage to portray. . . . It's the picture of Christ and the church."[2]

The monogamous, lifelong union of the two sexes, and the family that results, has served as the bedrock of Christian civilization for centuries. Yet during the twentieth century, in only a few generations, sex, marriage, and the family have been radically deconstructed and redefined. Behaviors and "lifestyles" once commonly considered by church and state as an affront to human dignity and a serious threat to the social order not only are touted by the secular media as goods to be pursued but are now sanctioned by many churches and protected as legal "rights" by various governments around the world.

Have you ever wondered what brought about so radical a shift so quickly? Have you ever wondered how we have become so radically dis-oriented in these matters? The answer is complex, but, as Christians, we must have the courage to revisit something that happened in our past—something that played a significant role in setting us and, in turn, society at large on the slippery slope that has led to today's sexual chaos. Early in the twentieth century, as we'll learn below, we Christians renounced our own biblical heritage by parting from over nineteen hundred years of clear, firm, and uninterrupted Christian teaching about the God-given purpose of sex.

Allow me to quote Rick Warren one last time: "You cannot value something when you don't understand its purpose. Anytime we forget God's purpose for any of his gifts, that gift is going to be misused, abused, confused, wasted, perverted, and even destroyed."[3] Warren himself may not know how applicable his own words are to the difficult issue to which we must now turn our careful and prayerful attention. Even to present it as an issue is to provoke the ire of those who insist that it is a nonissue, as I once did. The costs—to our own personal lives, our marriages and families, our congregations, and society at large—of reconsidering this can just seem too staggeringly high. On the other hand, the costs of *not* taking an honest look at this issue may be even higher.

Based on all we have learned about the God-given theology of our bodies, we simply cannot neglect to ask this question: Does an intentionally sterilized act of intercourse image God's *free*, *total*, *faithful*, *fruitful* love, or does it miss the mark? If it misses the mark, in what direction does it shift us? Where does intentionally sterilized sex cause us to veer?

The First Break

Knowledge of our own history as Christians can have a powerfully expansive effect on our understanding of our faith. I remember, for example, how surprised I was to learn that, until 1930, all Christian denominations were unanimous in their firm opposition to any attempt to sterilize sexual intercourse (what might those Christians have understood for all those centuries that we have forgotten?). When the Anglican Church opened the door to contraception at its Lambeth Conference that year, it was the first Christian body to break with the continuous teaching of the early church, the spiritual masters throughout the ages, and all the Reformers from Luther to Calvin and beyond. By the time the pill debuted in the early 1960s, the historical Christian teaching, once universally held, had come to be seen as archaic and absurd.

Most Christians today see contraception as a given of modern life and even as the responsible thing for believers to do. At the same time, Christian leaders of various denominations are revisiting the question. Randy Alcorn writes:

> This is a tough issue, and the toughest part is that we've grown up in a society forged by people like Margaret Sanger, and the church has largely bought into a selfish, anti-child, population-control mentality. Hence, the average Christian never even asks the question—I didn't ask it until I'd been a pastor for fifteen years. No one ever suggested to me that birth control was even an issue, it was just a given. No pastor counseled us to evaluate birth control, no Christian book on preparing for marriage

(and we read a number of them) suggested we even search the Scriptures or pray about the subject. The only question was which method of contraception was best, never whether contraception was best. I confess I carried over the same mentality to my premarital counseling as a pastor.[4]

Albert Mohler writes, "I think the contraceptive revolution caught evangelicals by surprise. We bought into a mentality of human control . . . and just received the Pill as one more great medical advance." In retrospect, he observes that "the Pill has done more to reorder human life than any event since Adam and Eve ate the apple. Why? Because sex, sexuality, and reproduction are so central to human life, to marriage, and to the future of humanity." He concludes by observing that "evangelicals are joining the discussion about birth control and its meaning. Evangelicals arrived late to the issue of abortion, and we have arrived late to the issue of birth control, but we are here now. . . . Nothing of this significance should escape the thoughtful concern of faithful Christians."[5]

Tracing the Roots

Has the modern embrace of contraception really done more to reorder human life than anything since our first parents committed the original sin? Mohler's statement may be hyperbole, but it's certainly true that the sexual revolution of the twentieth century—and the resultant culture of death—is simply inexplicable apart from the nearly universal acceptance of contraception. In fact, when Planned Parenthood founder Margaret Sanger first started her global campaigns for contraception in the early 1900s, there was no shortage of predictions that embracing contraception would lead to the societal chaos in which we're now immersed. You might be just as surprised as I was to read what the following prominent thinkers of the early twentieth century had to say about contraception and what they predicted would happen if we embraced it.

Sigmund Freud, for example, while he was certainly no friend of religion, understood that the "abandonment of the reproductive function is the common feature of all perversions. We actually describe a sexual activity as perverse," he said, "if it has given up the aim of reproduction and pursues the attainment of pleasure as an aim independent of it."[6]

Theodore Roosevelt condemned contraception as a serious threat against the welfare of the nation, describing it as "the one sin for which the penalty is national death, race death; a sin for which there is no atonement."[7]

Mahatma Gandhi insisted that "there can be no two opinions about the necessity of birth-control. But the only [appropriate] method . . . is self-control," which he described as "an infallibly sovereign remedy doing good to those who practice it." On the other hand, "to seek to escape the consequences of one's acts" with contraception is a remedy that "will prove to be worse than the disease." Why? Because contraceptive methods are "like putting a premium on vice. They make men and women reckless. . . . Nature is relentless and will have full revenge for any such violation of her laws," he predicted. "Moral results can only be produced by moral restraints." Hence, if contraceptive methods "become the order of the day, nothing but moral degradation can be the result. . . . As it is, man has sufficiently degraded woman for his lust, and [contraception], no matter how well meaning the advocates may be, will still further degrade her."[8]

When a committee of the Federal Council of Churches in America issued a report suggesting it follow the Anglican accep-

tance of contraception, the *Washington Post* published a sting-
ing editorial with the following prophetic statement: "Carried
to its logical conclusions, the committee's report if carried into
effect would sound the death knell of marriage as a holy institution by establishing degrading practices which would encourage indiscriminate immorality. The suggestion that the use of
legalized contraceptives would be 'careful and restrained' is
preposterous."[9]

Also in response to the Anglican break with Christian moral
teaching, T. S. Eliot asserted, "The World is trying the experiment of attempting to form a civilized but non-Christian mentality. The experiment will fail; but we must be very patient in
waiting its collapse; meanwhile redeeming the time: so that
the Faith may be preserved alive through the dark ages before
us; to renew and rebuild civilization, and save the World from
suicide."[10]

Perversity? National death? Moral degradation? The death
of marriage as a holy institution? World suicide? Isn't that a
bit much to pin on contraception? It would certainly seem so,
if it weren't for the fact that so much of what these forecasters
predicted has indeed come to pass. What did they understand
that we have forgotten? Put simply: *genitals* are meant to *generate*, and a culture that fails to respect this truth will *de-generate*.
Let's explore why.

Untying the Tight-Knot Nexus

The biblical vision of sexuality as understood throughout the
ages can be summarized very simply: marriage, sex, and babies
belong together—and in that order. In his loving design, God
has united these three realities in a tight knot to reveal in our
flesh the truth of his own eternal covenant love and fatherhood.

Contraception not only loosens the knot of this fundamental and society-ordering nexus, it also cuts the ties.

Separate sex from babies and you also eventually separate sex from marriage—both in principle and in practice. So long as the natural connection between sex and babies is retained, we realize intuitively that sexual intercourse is the rightful domain of those who have committed themselves to raising children: that commitment is called marriage. Insert contraception into the tight-knot nexus of marriage, sex, and babies, and everything will start to unravel as follows.

The temptation to commit adultery is certainly nothing new. However, one of the main deterrents throughout history from succumbing to the temptation has been the fear of an unwanted pregnancy. That's the tight-knot nexus of marriage, sex, and babies doing its job. What would happen to rates of adultery in a given population if we untied that knot with contraception? Incidents of infidelity would be sure to rise. What happens when incidents of infidelity rise? Rates of marital breakdown and divorce rise.

It gets worse. The temptation to engage in sex before marriage is nothing new. However, one of the main deterrents throughout history from succumbing to the temptation has been the fear of unwanted pregnancy. Once again, that's the tight-knot nexus doing its job. What would happen to rates of fornication in a given population if we untied that knot with contraception? They would certainly rise.

It gets worse. Since no method of contraception is 100 percent effective, an increase in adultery and fornication in a given population will inevitably lead to an increase in unwanted pregnancies. What happens when large numbers of women find themselves pregnant and don't want to be? Demand for a legal "right" to abortion logically follows as a way of "solving" this problem.

The common wisdom is that better access to contraception decreases rates of abortion. That may be the case in given situations. However, once we've severed the knot uniting marriage, sex, and babies, we don't like it when nature's nexus reasserts itself. The initial impulse to indulge libido without commitment and without consequence now morphs into a *demand* to be "free" to do so, even at the cost of terminating an innocent human life. While there's an initial logic to the idea that contraception curbs abortion, when we take a deeper look we realize that trying to solve the latter with the former is like throwing gasoline on a fire to try to put it out. In the final analysis, there is only one reason we have abortion: because people who do not love one another *freely, totally, faithfully,* and *fruitfully* are having sex.

It gets worse. Not everyone will resort to abortion, of course. (Thanks be to God for that.) Some will offer their children up for adoption, a heroic decision. In most cases, however, the mothers will raise their children on their own. This, too, can be heroic, but now the number of children who grow up without a father—which has already increased with the rise in divorce—will be compounded. Certainly God's grace can supply what is lacking, and those raised without a father can lead healthy, holy lives. Still, as numerous studies (and common sense) indicate, growing up without a father dramatically increases the chances that children will experience poverty; have emotional, psychological, and behavioral issues; suffer poor health; drop out of school; engage in premarital sex; obtain abortions; do drugs; commit violent crimes; and end up in jail.[11] All of these social ills compound exponentially from generation to generation, since "fatherless" children are also much more likely to have out-of-wedlock births and, if they marry at all, divorce.

Redefining Marriage, Sex, and Babies

As history clearly shows, when we begin untying the tight-knot nexus of marriage, sex, and babies, we end up redefining all three. Babies become mere "clumps of cells." Sex becomes mere pleasure exchange between consenting partners (gender being irrelevant). And marriage becomes a demanded societal and governmental "stamp of approval" on one's preferred method of sexual pleasure exchange.

And this is why embracing contraception has led, as a matter of course, to the normalization of homosexual behavior. Pardon the frankness, but as a plain-talking professor of mine once put it, "As soon as you sever orgasm from procreation, any orifice will do." It's hard to argue with that logic. Deliberately sterilizing sexual intercourse effectively nullifies the natural and essential meaning of sexual difference. In other words, deliberately rendering the genitals unable to generate has the effect of nullifying the natural and essential meaning of gender. When we recognize this, we come to see a hard truth: Christians themselves unwittingly began to "homo-sexualize" marriage when they began to embrace contraception. When married couples claim a "right" to sterilize their union, it's only a matter of time before those inclined to inherently sterile unions (i.e., same-sex unions) claim a "right" to marry.

Seventy-two years after the 1930 Anglican decision, Archbishop of Canterbury Rowan Williams observed that "the absolute condemnation of same-sex relations" has nothing substantial to rely upon in "a church that accepts the legitimacy of contraception."[12] He was correct. But rather than question the legitimacy of contraception, he took that as a given and justified homosexual behavior. If we're being consistent, it's one or the other.

New Testament scholar Richard Hays, commenting on the famous passage from Romans 1, observes that the apostle Paul "portrays homosexual behavior as a kind of 'sacrament' (so to speak) of the anti-religion of human beings who refuse to honor God as Creator. When human beings engage in homosexual activity, they enact an outward and visible sign of an inward and spiritual reality: the rejection of the Creator's design."[13]

Can't the same be said about those who choose to sterilize sexual intercourse? To embrace God's *design* is to embrace the meaning *of the sign* (de-sign). This is where the logic of the theology of our bodies leads us: to a biblical understanding of sexuality that we could call the "ethics of the sign."

Ethics of the Sign

The traditional biblical vision of sexuality "is strictly linked with our earlier reflections about *marriage in the dimension of the (sacramental) sign*."[14] All of married life is meant to be a sign of God's life and love. But marriage has a consummate expression. Spouses signify God's love in an unspeakably profound way when they become one flesh. Here, like no other moment in married life, spouses are called to participate in the "profound mystery" of God's love. But this will only happen if their sexual union accurately signifies God's love. Therefore, as John Paul II concludes, we can speak of moral good and evil in the sexual relationship based on whether the couple gives to their union the character of a truthful sign.[15]

The essential element for marriage to be a *true sign* is the language of the body spoken in truth. By participating in God's eternal plan of love, the language of the body becomes "prophetic." Traditional Christian teaching against contraception simply carries this truth to its logical conclusions.

147

What happens to the prophetic language of the body when it's overlaid with contraception? Are spouses true or false prophets in such a case? Is their union a true sign of the "profound mystery" of Christ's love for the church? What kind of theology are they now proclaiming with their bodies? Are they proclaiming the mystery of the God who has revealed himself as eternal *Father*? Or have they exchanged the truth of God for a lie (see Rom. 1:25)?

During conjugal intercourse, a "*moment so rich in meaning, it is . . . particularly important that the 'language of the body' be re-read in truth.*"[16] The language of the body has clear-cut meanings, all of which are "programmed" in the traditional vows of Christian marriage. For example, to "the question: 'Are you ready to accept children lovingly from God . . . ?' the man and the woman answer, 'Yes.'"[17]

If spouses say yes at the altar but then render their union sterile, are they being faithful to their wedding vows? Someone might retort, "Come on! I can commit to being open to children at the altar, but this doesn't mean *each and every* act of intercourse needs to be open to children." That was one of my objections when I first started considering these issues. And it sure seems to make sense. But what happens when we apply the same logic to the other promises of marriage? "Come on! I can commit to fidelity at the altar, but this doesn't mean *each and every* act of intercourse needs to be with my spouse." Really? Does fidelity most of the time justify adultery every once in a while? I had to admit that if I could recognize the inconsistency of a commitment to fidelity . . . *but not always*, then I could also recognize the inconsistency of a commitment to being open to children . . . *but not always*.

Looking for another way out of this logic, I thought a couple might simply exclude openness to children in the commitment they make at the altar. Then a couple's contracepted acts of intercourse wouldn't contradict their commitment. True, but God's love is *generous*; it *generates*. And that's why God made us *gendered* creatures with *genitals*: to image his *generous*, *generating* love. To exclude openness to life in a couple's commitment would not be to love as God loves, and it would not be Christian marriage. (It shouldn't come as a surprise that the modern embrace of contraception in our churches has, indeed, led many denominations to rewrite the traditional vows of Christian marriage, sometimes excluding all mention of children, essentially redefining marriage itself.)

What Shall We Do?

On the day of Pentecost, when Peter unfolded the Scriptures for all those gathered in Jerusalem, those who had been oblivious to the identity of the man they recently crucified "were cut to the heart and said to Peter and the other apostles, 'Brothers, what shall we do?' Peter replied, 'Repent'" (Acts 2:37–38).

In my experience, when the reasons for the traditional Christian teaching against contraception are properly laid out and the history and repercussions of embracing contraception are clearly unfolded, those believers who had been oblivious to the seriousness of the matter have their own kind of Peter's speech moment: "What shall we do?" Perhaps it's time for us as believers to reckon with what we have done by parting from our own Christian heritage. And perhaps it's time to reform our ways.

"What shall we do?" is a pressing question in the practical realm of married life as well. Suppose a couple comes to the conviction that the historical Christian teaching against contraception isn't crazy after all. Does fidelity to this teaching mean couples have no recourse but to let the babies come one after another? Some Christians believe that any attempt to limit or space births demonstrates a lack of trust in God's providence.[18]

We are, of course, called to trust in God's providence in all things. Reason is part of God's providence, however, and he expects us to use it. Recall that Christ rebuked Satan's attempt to have him rely on God's providence in an unreasonable way, saying, "Do not put the Lord your God to the test" (Luke 4:12).

There are a host of potential situations in married life when it seems clear that bringing another child into the world would be putting God's providence to the test: poor health, financial hardship, emotional or psychological difficulties. What could a couple do in these situations that would not violate the sign of God's love? In other words, what could they do to avoid conceiving a child that would not involve sterilizing their union? I'll bet you a million dollars you're doing it at this very moment. They could *abstain* from sex. For nearly two thousand years, all Christian denominations taught that the only method of *birth control* in keeping with human dignity is *self-control*. Perhaps they (along with Gandhi) were correct.

Does this mean a couple would need to abstain from sex until after their childbearing years? Let's think it through. A couple past their childbearing years is a good case in point. They know that their union will not result in a child. Are they violating "the sign" if they engage in intercourse with this knowledge? Are they rejecting God's design? No. They are *accepting* God's design. The Creator has also designed a woman's fertility cycle so that during her childbearing years she is naturally infertile for about three weeks out of every month. Properly trained in what modern science has learned about the signs of fertility, couples can know when they are fertile and when they are infertile. If a couple has a serious reason to avoid a pregnancy, they can abstain when they're fertile. If they so desire, they can embrace when they are naturally infertile without violating the Creator's design.

Employing this approach is often called "natural family planning" (NFP) or "fertility awareness method" (FAM). It's an approach growing in popularity among Christians of various denominations certainly for moral reasons but also simply because it's organic and in no way alters the body and its normal, natural functioning. Readers unfamiliar with modern methods of NFP should note that any woman, regardless of the regularity of her cycles, can use it successfully. In fact, modern methods of NFP are 98–99 percent effective in allowing couples to space or avoid pregnancy. This is not the outdated and much-less-effective "rhythm method."

To some, this seems like splitting hairs. "What's the big difference," they ask, "between rendering the union sterile yourself and just *waiting* until it's naturally infertile? The end result is the same thing: both couples avoid children." Well, we might ask, "What's the big difference between killing Grandma and just *waiting* until she dies naturally? The end result is the same thing: dead Grandma." Yes, the end result is the same thing, but one is a serious sin called murder, while in the other case, Grandma dies, but there's no sin involved whatsoever. Give it some thought: if we can see a significant difference between euthanasia and natural death, we can see a significant difference between contraception and natural family planning.

First, it's important to realize that the traditional Christian view does not say that it's inherently wrong to avoid children. The end (avoiding children), however, does not justify the means. There may well be a good reason for you to wish Grandma would pass on to the next life. Perhaps she is suffering terribly with age and disease. But this does not justify killing her. Similarly, you may have a good reason to avoid conceiving a child. But if the Christian teaching passed down through the ages is correct, no scenario justifies rendering the sexual act sterile.

My point here is not to suggest that rendering sex sterile is the same thing as murder (one impedes a life from coming to be while the other takes a life that already exists). Rather, my point is to explore whether in both cases we aren't rejecting our status as creatures and playing God. Grandma's natural death and a woman's natural period of infertility are both acts of God. But in killing Grandma and in rendering sex sterile, are we not taking the powers of life into our own hands—just as the deceiver originally tempted us to do—and making ourselves like God (see Gen. 3:5)?

Love or Lust?

One of the main objections to the historical teaching against contraception is that abstinence impedes couples from expressing their love for one another. Let's take a closer look at this point.

First of all, it's true that abstaining from sex for the wrong reasons (out of spite for a spouse; out of disdain for sex, etc.) is damaging to marital love. But, as every married couple knows, abstaining from sex for the right reasons is a profound act of love. Indeed, there are many occasions in married life when a couple might *want* to renew their vows through intercourse but love demands that they abstain: maybe one of the spouses is sick; maybe it's after childbirth; maybe they're at the in-laws and there are thin walls; or maybe the couple has a serious reason to avoid a child. In these cases, and in many others, if a couple *can't* abstain, their love is called into question.

What purpose does contraception really serve? This might sound odd at first, but give it some thought: contraception was not actually invented to prevent pregnancy. We already had a 100 percent safe, 100 percent reliable way of doing that: it's called *abstinence*. In the final analysis, contraception serves one purpose: to circumvent our lack of self-control. In other words, when all the smoke is cleared, it would appear that the real reason contraception exists is to serve the indulgence of lust. And the Bible is unambiguous on this point: "It is God's will that . . . each of you should learn to control your own body in a way that is holy and honorable, not in passionate lust like the pagans, who do not know God. . . . The Lord will punish all those who commit such sins, as we told you and warned you before. For God did not call us to be impure, but to live a holy life. Therefore, anyone who rejects this instruction does not reject a human being but God" (1 Thess. 4:3–8).

Why do we spay or neuter our dogs and cats? Why don't we just ask them to abstain? Because they cannot say no to their urge to merge; they're not free. If we spay and neuter ourselves through contraception, are we not reducing the "profound mystery" of the one-flesh union to the level of Fido and Fidette in heat? What distinguished us from the animals in the first place (remember original solitude)? *Freedom*—and the responsibility that comes with it. God gave us freedom as the capacity to love. If we cannot say no to sex, what does our yes mean? Only the person who is *free* with the freedom for which Christ set us free (see Gal. 5:1) is capable of authentic love.

In reality, what we often call love, "if subjected to searching critical examination turns out to be, contrary to all appearances, only a form of 'utilization' of the person."[19] To overcome this utilitarian attitude toward sex and learn the art of loving "as Christ loves" demands that we do battle with our fallen sexual instincts. As C. S. Lewis observed, the biblical vision of sexual morality is "so contrary to our instincts, that obviously either Christianity is wrong or our sexual instinct, as it now is, has gone wrong. One or the other."[20] Until 1930, all Christian denominations were in agreement that it was the sexual instinct that was in need of reform, not the Christian vision of sexuality. That year, it would seem we started reforming the Christian vision of sexuality to conform to our disordered instincts. And can we not now recognize the incredibly high price we've paid for doing so?

Sexual Purity and the Integration of Love

One often hears it said in Christian circles that we need to stay pure *until* we get married, as if married people don't need any sexual virtue. But this is to equate purity with saying no to our sexual desires. Purity *does* say no to disordered sexual desires, but it also frees sexual desire from "the utilitarian attitude," from the tendency to *use* others for our own gratification, so that we can learn the art of self-giving love. From this perspective, sexual purity is an absolute requirement of spouses, lest we degrade marriage to a "legitimate outlet" for the indulgence of lust. Sexual purity requires ongoing training in *self-mastery* so that we are in control of our sexual desires and not vice versa.

As we learned earlier, self-mastery does not merely mean resisting unruly desires by force of will. That's only the negative side of the picture. As we develop self-mastery, we experience it as the ability to orient sexual reactions, in terms of both their content and their character.[21] The person who is truly pure is able to direct erotic desire "toward what is true, good, and beautiful, so that what is 'erotic' also becomes true, good, and

154

beautiful."[22] As spouses experience liberation from lust, they enter into the freedom of the gift that enables them to express the language of their bodies "in a depth, simplicity, and beauty hitherto altogether unknown."[23]

It's certainly true that purity requires self-denial, understood as a ready and determined willingness to resist the impulses of lust. But remember, Christian purity does not repress. It enters into Christ's death and resurrection. As lust dies, authentic love is raised up. Paraphrasing John Paul II, if purity manifests itself at first as an ability to resist lust, as it matures it reveals itself as a singular ability to perceive, love, and experience the "language of the body" in a way that remains completely unknown to lust.[24] Hence, the discipline required by purity does not impoverish or impede a couple's expressions of love and affection. Rather, like a musician who disciplines himself to make more beautiful music, the discipline required of purity makes a couple's expressions of love "spiritually more intense and thus *enriches* them."[25]

Marital Spirituality

Purity, understood in this way, stands at the center of the spirituality of marriage. What is "marital spirituality"? It's living according to God's in-spiration in married life. It involves spouses opening themselves to the indwelling power of the Holy Spirit and allowing him to guide them in all their choices and behaviors. John Paul II observes that sexual union itself—with all its emotional joys and physical pleasures—is meant to be an expression of "life according to the Holy Spirit."[26] When spouses are open to the gift, the Holy Spirit infuses them "with everything that is noble and beautiful," with "the supreme value which is love."[27] But when spouses close themselves off to the

Holy Spirit, sexual union quickly degenerates into an act of selfishness and lust, an act of mutual exploitation.

Apart from the Holy Spirit, human weakness makes the traditional Christian teaching on sexual morality a burden that no one can bear. But to whom is this teaching given? To men and women enslaved by their weaknesses? Or to men and women set free by the power of the Holy Spirit? If we are to uphold the historic teaching of Christianity on sexual morality, we can do so only with absolute confidence in the fact that "God's love has been poured out into our hearts through the Holy Spirit, who has been given to us" (Rom. 5:5).

John Paul II observes that life in the Holy Spirit leads spouses to understand, among all the possible manifestations of love and affection, "the singular, and even exceptional meaning" of the sexual embrace.[28] Spouses who open their union to the Holy Spirit are filled with a profound "reverence for what comes from God" that shapes their spirituality *"for the sake of protecting the particular dignity of [the sexual] act."*[29] Such spouses understand that their union is meant to signify and participate in God's creative and redeeming love. In other words, they understand the theology of their bodies. And being filled with a deep "veneration for *the essential values of conjugal union"* makes them sensitive to anything that even hints of "violating or degrading what bears in itself the sign of the divine mystery of creation and redemption."[30]

Perhaps we've not been sensitive to the fact that joining in one flesh is a "sign of the divine mystery of creation and redemption." Perhaps we've been caught up in a thousand lies about the meaning of our bodies and our sexuality. But it doesn't matter how dyslexic or even illiterate we may have been in reading the divine language of the body up to this point in our lives. As John Paul II boldly proclaims, through the gift of redemption there is always the possibility of passing from error to the truth; there is always the possibility of conversion from sin to sexual purity as an expression of life according to the Spirit.[31]

> *Come, Holy Spirit, come! Convert our hearts from lust to love. Impregnate our sexual desires with divine passion so that, loving as God loves on earth, we might one day rejoice in the consummation of the marriage of the Lamb in heaven. Amen.*

CONCLUSION

At the *core* of [the] Gospel . . . is the affirmation of the inseparable connection between the person, his life and his bodiliness.

—John Paul II

"The Word became flesh and made his dwelling among us"
(John 1:14). "Word" doesn't quite convey all the richness of the
Greek *logos*, which refers to the rational principle governing
the universe—the ultimate "meaning," "reason," and "logic"
behind *everything*. The astounding claim upon which all of
Christianity is based is that that Meaning has communicated
itself by taking on *flesh*. In this study of Sacred Scripture, we've
done nothing other than examine how the incarnation illuminates our own incarnate humanity as male and female. The
enfleshment of Ultimate Meaning becomes the ultimate "en-
meaning-ment" of the flesh. It is this: to reveal, communicate,
and enable us to "participate in the divine nature" (2 Pet. 1:4).

Human flesh—yours and mine—conveys not only *a* word
from God but *the* Word *of* God: "The Word became flesh and
made his dwelling among us" (John 1:14). This is why our

bodies, as we have learned throughout this study of God's Word, are not only *bio*-logical but *theo*-logical: they reveal the logic of God, the *Logos* of God. They reveal, proclaim, communicate the Word of God. Indeed, our bodies proclaim the gospel of Jesus Christ, which is always "the gospel of the body"—the gospel of the Word, the *Logos* (Ultimate Meaning) made flesh.

Much is at stake in the rampant confusion, both in the secular world and in our churches, about the meaning of the body, sexuality, gender, marriage, and the family. As one of my theological mentors, the late Lorenzo Albacete, observed:

> When [the gospel] is lacking in a person or in a culture, the barometer where its lack is most clearly seen is the attitude towards the body. . . . Indeed, . . . it is the desperate confusion and disarray with respect to human bodiliness, as shown in human sexuality, that shows the need for evangelization. . . . This absolutely inseparable relation between the Gospel and the experience of the body . . . can be seen in the fact that from the very beginning the *greatest* enemy of the Gospel has been the attempt to separate Jesus Christ from the flesh [see 2 John 1:7]. . . . The whole heart, the scandal, the newness, the *stunning* wonder of the Christian proposal . . . is that the Word—the Logos, Meaning, Sense, Beauty, Truth, Goodness, Destiny—has become flesh. The person who accepts [this] . . . knows that an attack against the body . . . is an attack against the very secret of God's life. And so that person develops a passion, a passion to come to the help of suffering bodies. . . . That sensitivity is in the end the decisive proof that evangelization has occurred.[1]

This suffering abounds in our post–sexual revolution world. If the essential goal of the sexual revolution was to sever the natural link between gender and the generation of human life, the goal now is to sever the natural link between human life

160

and gender itself. Despite all claims of "liberation" and the supposed triumph of "human rights," a de-gendered world can only de-generate.

Both steps, both ruptures in our humanity—the rupture of gender from life and the rupture of life from gender—are rooted in a gnostic/Manichaean view of the person in which body and soul are put in radical opposition. Severed from spiritual reality, we no longer experience the body, sexuality, and fertility as a "profound mystery." Instead, we come to experience them as a "profound misery." In turn, we experience gender (recall that "gender" means "the manner in which one is designed to generate") no longer as something to revere but instead as something to reject.

When we fail to appreciate the profound unity of body and soul, we no longer see the human body in light of our creation in the image and likeness of God. Rather, we reduce it to a thing to be used, exploited, manipulated, and even discarded at will, forgetting that that body is not just *a* body but *some*body. Within this milieu, as John Paul II observed, the human being *"ceases to live as a person and a subject. Regardless of all intentions and declarations to the contrary, he becomes merely an object."* Tragically, John Paul II continues, we have lost

the basis of that *primordial wonder* which led Adam on the morning of creation to exclaim before Eve: "This at last is bone of my bones and flesh of my flesh" (Gen. 2:23). This same wonder is echoed in the words of the Song of Solomon: "You have ravished my heart, my sister, my bride, you have ravished my heart with a glance of your eyes" (Song 4:9). How far removed are some modern ideas from the profound understanding of masculinity and femininity found in Divine Revelation! Revelation leads us to discover in *human sexuality a treasure proper to the person*, who finds true fulfillment in [marriage and] the family but who can likewise express his profound calling . . . in celibacy for the sake of the kingdom of God.[2]

We are living in dark times indeed, but let us never forget that "the light shines in the darkness, and the darkness has not overcome it" (John 1:5). We are people of hope, and the Bridegroom is preparing a great springtime for his bride (see Song 2:11–13). How do we pass over from this winter to the promised springtime? If we can recognize in the above the diagnosis of what ails the modern world, we can also recognize the cure. Here it is: We must recover a sense of *primordial wonder* at the divinely inspired beauty of the human body. We must come to recognize in the human body the revelation of the human *person* whose dignity demands that he or she never be used, exploited, manipulated, or discarded. We must rediscover the *treasure* of human sexuality and gender as a stupendous sign of the divine image in our humanity and as an invitation to use our freedom to live this divine image through the sincere gift of one's life in marriage or in celibacy for the kingdom. And we can do all of the above precisely by pondering the profound understanding of masculinity and femininity found in the Bible, found in God's Word *made flesh* in Jesus, the Christ.

This is what John Paul II's Theology of the Body provides. And you are now part of a microscopic percentage of people on this planet who have been exposed to it. What will you do with that responsibility? What will you do with the seeds that have fallen to you? I appeal to you, do not let the birds of the air eat them. Do not let the seeds die for lack of moisture. Do not let the cares of this world choke them off (see Luke 8:4–15). Tend to the soil and water the seeds by taking up a further, more in-depth study of the Theology of the Body. Here are a few suggestions on how you can continue your journey:

- Consider joining a worldwide online community of men and women who are receiving ongoing formation. Learn more by visiting theologyofthebody.com.
- If you have the aptitude, I encourage you to read John Paul II's actual text *Man and Woman He Created Them: A Theology of the Body.* If you need help with his scholarly approach, you could read it in conjunction with my extended commentary, *Theology of the Body Explained.*
- Visit theologyofthebody.com and click on "Shop" for a listing of various books and additional resources.
- Explore what other authors have written. There are many good resources offered by different teachers with their own emphases and insights. Search online for "theology of the body resources" and start exploring.
- Consider taking a five-day immersion course through the Theology of the Body Institute. Learn more at theologyofthebody.com.

If the Theology of the Body provides the answer to the crisis of our time, it's not because it offers the world some "profound teaching." Rather, it's because it reconnects the modern world with the "profound mystery" that is Christ and his love for his bride, the church. "We are certainly not seduced by the naive expectation that, faced with the great challenges of our time, we shall find some magic formula. No, we shall not be saved by a formula, but by a Person, and the assurance which he gives us: *I am with you!*"[3]

Christ the Bridegroom is with us, and he is "coming soon" in all his glory (see Rev. 22:7). This is what enables us to endure all that is happening in our world right now. The meaning of the body, sexuality, gender, marriage, and the family is being put on trial, condemned, mocked, rejected, spat upon, scourged, and crucified. But give it "three days" and watch what happens: "On the third day a wedding took place at Cana" (John 2:1). Jesus is always about the business of restoring God's wine to man and woman's relationship! This is our living hope. This is the hope offered in the Theology of the Body. If we share this hope with the world, we shall not fall short of renewing the face of the earth.

> The Spirit and the bride say, "Come!" And let the one who hears say, "Come!" Let the one who is thirsty come; and let the one who wishes take the free gift of the water of life. (Rev. 22:17)

ACKNOWLEDGMENTS

My thanks to Glenn Stanton, Mike Metzger, John Seel, Katie Tyndall, Paul Leland, Tory Baucum (especially for the Luther reference), Richard Marks, Spencer Mielki, Tim Sisarich, Andrew Franklin, Sam and Mary Kay Andreades, and Daniel Weiss—all of whom read drafts of the manuscript and offered constructive feedback.

I'd also like to thank my literary agent Mark Oestreicher ("Mark-O") for connecting me with all of the fine people at Baker and Brazos Press. I've worked with many good publishers over the years, but none have been as helpful, thorough, and professional as Brazos.

NOTES

Introduction

1. Christopher West, *Fill These Hearts: God, Sex, and the Universal Longing* (New York: Image, 2013), 23.

2. Quoted in Joseph Jalsavec, "A Baptist's Opposition to Contraception," *The Interim*, August 18, 2010, http://www.theinterim.com/issues/marriage-family/a-baptist%E2%80%99s-opposition-to-contraception.

Chapter 1: Our Bodies Tell God's Story

1. George Weigel, *Witness to Hope: The Biography of Pope John Paul II* (New York: HarperCollins, 1999), 343, 853.

2. John Paul II, *Man and Woman He Created Them: A Theology of the Body* (Boston: Pauline Books, 2006), 46:6. Hereafter *TOB*.

3. *TOB* 69:8.

4. *TOB* 49:3.

5. *TOB* 102:5.

6. C. S. Lewis, *Mere Christianity* (New York: HarperOne, 1952), 64.

7. *TOB* 45:3.

8. Lewis, *Mere Christianity*, 98.

9. Matthew Lee Anderson, *Earthen Vessels: Why Our Bodies Matter to Our Faith* (Minneapolis: Bethany House, 2011), 31.

10. *TOB* 23:4.

11. *TOB* 19:4.

12. *TOB* 40:4.

13. Dennis Kinlaw, *Let's Start with Jesus* (Grand Rapids: Zondervan, 2005), 28–29.

14. Kinlaw, *Let's Start with Jesus*, 13.

15. John Paul II, *Mulieris Dignitatem*, apostolic letter, August 15, 1988, §26, http://w2.vatican.va/content/john-paul-ii/en/apost_letters/1988/documents/hf_jp-ii_apl_15081988_mulieris-dignitatem.html.

16. See *TOB* 95b:1.

17. John Dillenberger, ed., *Martin Luther: Selections from His Writings* (New York: Anchor, 1962), 60.

18. Nicholas Cabasilas, *La vie en Jesus Christ* [Life in Jesus Christ], 2nd ed. (Chevetogne, 1960), 153.

19. Augustine of Hippo, *Sermo Suppositus* 120:3 (my translation).

20. See *TOB* 87:3.

21. *TOB* 87:6.

22. John Paul II, *Mulieris Dignitatem*, §26.

23. *TOB* 115:2.

24. John Paul II, *Letter to Families*, February 2, 1994, §23, http://w2.vatican.va /content/john-paul-ii/en/letters/1994/documents/hf_jp-ii_let_02021994_families.html.

25. Karol Wojtyla, *Love and Responsibility* (San Francisco: Ignatius, 1993), 66.

26. John Paul II, *Evangelium Vitae*, encyclical letter, March 25, 1995, §97, http:// w2.vatican.va/content/john-paul-ii/en/encyclicals/documents/hf_jp-ii_enc_2503199 5_evangelium-vitae.html.

Chapter 2: Sex in the Garden of Eden

1. Jessica Guynn, "Facebook's New Gender Option: Fill in the Blank," *USA Today*, February 26, 2015, https://www.usatoday.com/story/tech/2015/02/26/facebook-gender -option-fill-in-the-blank/24059551.

2. Karol Wojtyla, *Love and Responsibility* (San Francisco: Ignatius, 1993), 47.

3. *TOB* 11:1.

4. Christopher West, *Theology of the Body Explained: A Commentary on John Paul II's "Man and Woman He Created Them"* (Boston: Pauline Books and Media, 2007).

5. *TOB* 7:2.

6. *TOB* 9:3.

7. Tim Keller, "The Gospel and Sex," accessed November 20, 2018, http://www.christ 2rculture.com/resources/Ministry-Blog/The-Gospel-and-Sex-by-Tim-Keller.pdf.

8. *TOB* 13:1.

9. *TOB* 15:1.

10. *TOB* 19:5.

11. *TOB* 15:1.

12. *TOB* 15:1.

13. *TOB* 15:5.

14. *TOB* 18:4.

15. *TOB* 15:5.

Chapter 3: The Fall and Redemption of Sex

1. Father Raniero Cantalamessa, "The Two Faces of Love," First Lenten Sermon to the Roman Curia, March 25, 2011, https://zenit.org/articles/father-cantalamessa-s -1st-lenten-sermon-2.

2. *TOB* 115:5.

3. See *TOB* 45:3.

4. *TOB* 51n61.

5. *TOB* 48:1.

6. *TOB* 43:7.
7. *TOB* 43:2.
8. *TOB* 33:2.
9. *TOB* 43:5.
10. See *TOB* 25:2.
11. See *TOB* 46:6.
12. Dallas Willard, *The Divine Conspiracy: Rediscovering Our Hidden Life in God* (New York: HarperOne, 1997), 35–59.
13. Dallas Willard, *The Great Omission: Reclaiming Jesus's Essential Teachings on Discipleship* (New York: HarperOne, 2014), 34.
14. *TOB* 20:1.
15. *TOB* 32:6.
16. See *TOB* 29:4.
17. See *TOB* 40:4.
18. *TOB* 28:3.
19. *TOB* 27:1.
20. *TOB* 45:3.
21. John Paul II, *Dominum et Vivificantem*, encyclical letter, May 18, 1986, §51, http://w2.vatican.va/content/john-paul-ii/en/encyclicals/documents/hf_jp-ii_enc_180 51986_dominum-et-vivificantem.html.
22. See *TOB* 46:5.
23. *TOB* 46:5.
24. See *TOB* 43:6.
25. Karol Wojtyla, *Love and Responsibility* (San Francisco: Ignatius, 1993), 170–71.
26. John Paul II, *Veritatis Splendor*, encyclical letter, August 6, 1993, §15, http://w2.vatican.va/content/john-paul-ii/en/encyclicals/documents/hf_jp-ii_enc_0608199 3_veritatis-splendor.html.
27. *TOB* 58:7.
28. *TOB* 57:3.
29. Alexander Men, *Son of Man: The Story of Christ and Christianity* (Oosterhout, Netherlands: Oakwood, 1998), 93.
30. John Paul II, "Celebration of the Unveiling of the Restorations of Michelangelo's Frescos in the Sistine Chapel," homily, April 8, 1994, §6, http://w2.vatican.va/content/john-paul-ii/en/homilies/1994/documents/hf_jp-ii_hom_19940408_restauri-sistina.html.
31. *TOB* 63:5.
32. *TOB* 63:5.
33. John Paul II, *Veritatis Splendor*, §103.
34. Wojtyla, *Love and Responsibility*, 190–91.
35. *TOB* 46:4.
36. *TOB* 46:6.
37. *TOB* 128:1.
38. C. S. Lewis, *The Great Divorce* (New York: Macmillan, 1946), 104.
39. *TOB* 32:3.
40. *TOB* 129:5.
41. *TOB* 48:1.
42. *TOB* 117b:5.
43. *TOB* 48:4.

Chapter 4: Will There Be Sex in Heaven?

1. Matthew Lee Anderson, *Earthen Vessels: Why Our Bodies Matter to Our Faith* (Minneapolis: Bethany House, 2011), 38, citing N. T. Wright, *Surprised by Hope* (New York: HarperCollins, 2008).
2. *TOB* 66:6.
3. Peter Kreeft, *Everything You Ever Wanted to Know about Heaven* (San Francisco: Ignatius, 1990), 93.
4. *TOB* 67:1.
5. Rick Warren, "The Biblical Meaning of Marriage," address at Humanum Colloquium, November 18, 2014.
6. Dennis Kinlaw, *Let's Start with Jesus* (Grand Rapids: Zondervan, 2005), 62.
7. C. S. Lewis, *The Weight of Glory* (New York: HarperCollins, 2001), 26.
8. Tim Keller, "The Gospel and Sex," accessed November 20, 2018, http://www.christ2rculture.com/resources/Ministry-Blog/The-Gospel-and-Sex-by-Tim-Keller.pdf.
9. Karol Wojtyla, *Love and Responsibility* (San Francisco: Ignatius, 1993), 255.
10. Anderson, *Earthen Vessels*, 131.
11. *TOB* 75:1.
12. Lewis, *The Weight of Glory*, 42.
13. *TOB* 68:4.
14. *TOB* 15:1.
15. *TOB* 67:3.
16. See *TOB* 69:5.
17. *TOB* 75:1.
18. Keller, "The Gospel and Sex."
19. John Eldredge, *The Journey of Desire* (Nashville: Nelson, 2000), 141–42.
20. John Paul II, *Novo Millennio Ineunte*, apostolic letter, January 6, 2001, §33, http://w2.vatican.va/content/john-paul-ii/en/apost_letters/2001/documents/hf_jp-ii_apl_20010106_novo-millennio-ineunte.html.
21. John Paul II, *Novo Millennio Ineunte*, §33.

Chapter 5: This Is a Profound Mystery

1. *TOB* 79:6.
2. Karol Wojtyla, *Love and Responsibility* (San Francisco: Ignatius, 1993), 140.
3. *TOB* 92:3.
4. *TOB* 95b:7.
5. *TOB* 87:6.
6. John Paul II, *Letter to Families*, February 2, 1994, §19, http://w2.vatican.va/content/john-paul-ii/en/letters/1994/documents/hf_jp-ii_let_02021994_families.html.
7. *TOB* 87:3, 6.
8. *TOB* 95:7.
9. *TOB* 89:7.
10. *TOB* 89:5, 6.
11. *TOB* 89:3, 4.
12. See *TOB* 90:2; 89:4.
13. *TOB* 117b:4.
14. *TOB* 58:7.
15. *TOB* 90:2.

16. *TOB* 92:6.

17. Wojtyla, *Love and Responsibility*, 272, 275.

18. *TOB* 90:2.

19. John Paul II, *Mulieris Dignitatem*, apostolic letter, August 15, 1988, §27, http://w2.vatican.va/content/john-paul-ii/en/apost_letters/1988/documents/hf_jp-ii_apl_15081988_mulieris-dignitatem.html.

20. See *TOB* 95:7.

21. *TOB* 97:2.

22. John Paul II, *Redemptor Hominis*, encyclical letter, March 4, 1979, §1, http://w2.vatican.va/content/john-paul-ii/en/encyclicals/documents/hf_jp-ii_enc_04031979_redemptor-hominis.html.

23. *TOB* 96:5.

24. *TOB* 93:1.

25. *TOB* 91:8.

26. *TOB* 96:6; 19:4.

27. See *TOB* 93:5.

28. *TOB* 97:4.

29. *TOB* 97:5.

30. See *TOB* 95b:7.

31. *TOB* 102:5.

Chapter 6: Sex Refers to Christ and His Church

1. *TOB* 13:1.

2. See Karol Wojtyla, *Love and Responsibility* (San Francisco: Ignatius, 1993), 135.

3. While few outside the Orthodox and Catholic churches consider Tobit a canonical book of the Bible and thus as decisive for doctrine, various Protestant denominations still recognize the wisdom of this ancient book and recommend reading it "for example of life" (Thirty-Nine Articles of the Church of England, art. 6). It is precisely "for example of life" that we turn to the marriage of Tobias and Sarah.

4. Christopher West, *Fill These Hearts: God, Sex, and the Universal Longing* (New York: Image, 2013), 87–89.

5. *TOB* 123:4.

6. *TOB* 103:2.

7. *TOB* 103:3.

8. Tim Keller, "The Gospel and Sex," accessed November 20, 2018, http://www.christ2rculture.com/resources/Ministry-Blog/The-Gospel-and-Sex-by-Tim-Keller.pdf.

9. See *TOB* 106:4.

10. *TOB* 115:2, 3.

11. Melinda Selmys, "Divorce: In the Image and Likeness of Hell," *National Catholic Register*, September 25, 2007, http://www.ncregister.com/site/article/divorce_in_the_image_and_likeness_of_hell.

12. Keller, "The Gospel and Sex."

13. Gregory, *Homilies on the Song of Songs* 1, in Richard A. Norris, trans. and ed., *The Song of Songs as Interpreted by Early Christian and Medieval Commentators* (Grand Rapids: Eerdmans, 2003), 18.

14. *TOB* 108nn95, 97.

15. *TOB* 108n96.

16. *TOB* 108n97.

17. *TOB* 110:1.

18. *TOB* 110:1.

19. *TOB* 110:2.

20. C. S. Lewis, *Mere Christianity* (New York: HarperOne, 1952), 98.

21. *TOB* 110:8.

22. *TOB* 110:7.

23. See *TOB* 110:7.

24. *TOB* 111:4.

25. *TOB* 109:2.

26. *TOB* 111:5.

27. *TOB* 111:6.

28. See note 3 above.

29. *TOB* 111:6.

30. *TOB*, p. 597 (page number supplied in lieu of audience number).

31. *TOB*, p. 601.

32. See *TOB* 116:2.

33. *TOB* 115:2.

34. *TOB* 117:2.

35. See *TOB* 116:5.

36. John Paul II, *Familiaris Consortio*, apostolic exhortation, November 22, 1981, §13, http://w2.vatican.va/content/john-paul-ii/en/apost_exhortations/documents/hf_jp-ii_exh_19811122_familiaris-consortio.html.

37. Christopher West, *Heaven's Song: Sexual Love as It Was Meant to Be* (West Chester, PA: Ascension, 2008), 130.

38. *TOB* 12:5n22.

Chapter 7: Keeping God in the Bedroom

1. Rick Warren, interview by Raymond Arroyo, *World Over*, November 20, 2014, https://youtu.be/Pzw8rzldRMs (emphasis added).

2. Rick Warren, "The Biblical Meaning of Marriage," address at Humanum Colloquium, November 18, 2014.

3. Warren, "The Biblical Meaning of Marriage."

4. Randy Alcorn, "What Is Your View on Birth Control?," Eternal Perspective Ministries, February 15, 2010, https://www.epm.org/resources/2010/Feb/15/what-your-view-birth-control.

5. Quoted in Nancy Gibbs, "Love, Sex, Freedom, and the Paradox of the Pill," *Time*, May 3, 2010.

6. Sigmund Freud, *Introductory Lectures in Psychoanalysis* (New York: Norton, 1966), 392.

7. Theodore Roosevelt, *State Papers as Governor and President*, vol. 17 of *Works of Theodore Roosevelt*, National Edition, 20 vols. (New York: Charles Scribner's Sons, 1926), 442.

8. Mahatma Gandhi, *India of My Dreams* (New Delhi: Rajpal & Sons, 2009), 219–20.

9. "Forgetting Religion," *Washington Post*, March 22, 1931.

10. T. S. Eliot, "Thoughts after Lambeth," from *Selected Essays* (London: Faber 1972), 332.

11. For links to various studies on this issue, see Claudio Sanchez, "Poverty, Drop-outs, Pregnancy, Suicide: What The Numbers Say About Fatherless Kids," NPR, June 18, 2017, https://www.npr.org/sections/ed/2017/06/18/533062607/poverty-dropouts -pregnancy-suicide-what-the-numbers-say-about-fatherless-kids.

12. Rowan Williams, "The Body's Grace," in *Theology and Sexuality: Classic and Contemporary Readings*, ed. Eugene F. Rogers Jr. (Malden, MA: Blackwell, 2002), 320.

13. Richard Hays, *The Moral Vision of the New Testament: Community, Cross, New Creation* (New York: Harper, 1996), 386.

14. *TOB* 118:3.

15. See *TOB* 37:6.

16. *TOB* 118:4.

17. *TOB* 105:6; 106:3.

18. Google "Quiverfull," for example.

19. Karol Wojtyla, *Love and Responsibility* (San Francisco: Ignatius, 1993), 167.

20. C. S. Lewis, *Mere Christianity* (New York: HarperOne, 1952), 96.

21. See *TOB* 129:5.

22. *TOB* 48:1.

23. *TOB* 117b:5.

24. See *TOB* 128:3.

25. *TOB* 128:3.

26. See *TOB* 101:6.

27. *TOB* 46:5.

28. *TOB* 132:2.

29. *TOB* 132:2.

30. *TOB* 131:5.

31. See *TOB* 107:3.

Conclusion

1. Lorenzo Albacete, "Theology of the Body," lecture at University of San Francisco, Flocchini Forum, 1995.

2. John Paul II, *Letter to Families*, February 2, 1994, §19, http://w2.vatican.va /content/john-paul-ii/en/letters/1994/documents/hf_jp-ii_let_02021994_families.html.

3. John Paul II, *Novo Millennio Ineunte*, apostolic letter, January 6, 2001, §29, http://w2.vatican.va/content/john-paul-ii/en/apost_letters/2001/documents/hf_jp-ii _apl_20010106_novo-millennio-ineunte.html.

SCRIPTURE INDEX

SUBJECT INDEX

ABOUT THE AUTHOR

Christopher West is a proud husband and father of five. He also serves as president and senior lecturer for the Theology of the Body Institute near Philadelphia. His global presentations, bestselling books, and multiple audio and video programs have sparked an international groundswell of interest in John Paul II's Theology of the Body across denominational lines, and his work has been featured in the *New York Times* and on ABC News, Fox News, MSNBC, and countless Protestant and Catholic media outlets.